Reader's Handbook

A Student Guide for Reading and Learning

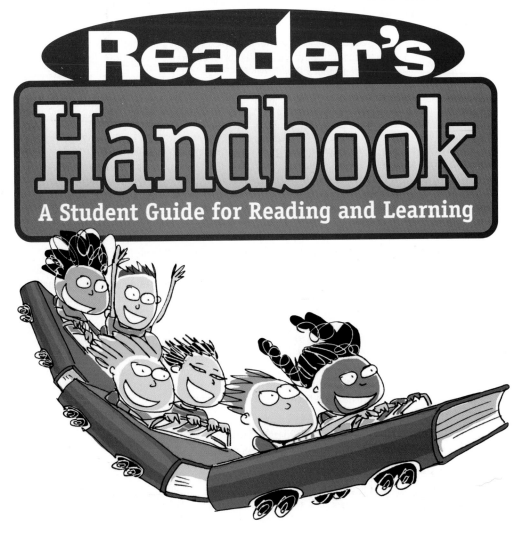

Great Source Education Group
a Houghton Mifflin Company
Wilmington, Massachusetts

www.greatsource.com

AUTHORS

Laura Robb
Author

Powhatan School, Boyce, Virginia

Laura Robb, author of *Teaching Reading in Middle School, Teaching Reading in Social Studies, Science, and Math, Redefining Staff Development,* and *Literacy Links,* has taught language arts at Powhatan School in Boyce, Virginia, for more than 35 years. She is a co-author of the *Reader's Handbooks* for grades 4–5 and 6–8, as well as the *Reading and Writing Sourcebooks* for grades 3–5 and the *Summer Success: Reading Program.* Robb also mentors and coaches teachers in Virginia public schools and speaks at conferences throughout the country.

April Nauman
Contributing Author

Northeastern Illinois University, Chicago, Illinois

April D. Nauman, Ph.D., is a teacher educator at Northeastern Illinois University in Chicago. For more than 10 years she has worked with Chicago area elementary and high school teachers to improve literacy instruction for their students, mostly in high-needs city schools. Dr. Nauman has authored many papers on literacy learning.

Donna Ogle
Contributing Author

National-Louis University, Evanston, Illinois

Donna M. Ogle, Professor of Reading and Language at National-Louis University in Evanston, Illinois, served as President of the International Reading Association 2001–2002. Her extensive staff development experiences include working in Russia and other eastern European countries as part of the Reading and Writing for Critical Thinking Project from 1999–2003. Her latest books are *Coming Together as Readers* (2001, Skylight Professional Books) and *Reading Comprehension: Strategies for Independent Learners,* co-authored with Camille Blachowicz (Guilford, 2000). She is also a senior consultant for McDougal Littell's history text, *Creating America* (2000).

Editorial: Developed by Nieman Inc. with Phil LaLeike

Design: Ronan Design: Sean O'Neill

Illustrations: Mike McConnell

Printed in the United States of America
International Standard Book Number: 0-669-51187-0 (hardcover)
1 2 3 4 5 6 7 8 9—RRDC—10 09 08 07 06 05 04
International Standard Book Number: 0-669-51188-9 (softcover)
1 2 3 4 5 6 7 8 9—RRDC—10 09 08 07 06 05 04

Consultants

Marilyn Crow
Wilmette Public Schools
Wilmette, IL

Ellen Fogelberg
Evanston Public Schools
Evanston, IL

Reviewers

Julie Anderson
Hawken Lower School
Lyndhurst, OH

Jay Brandon
JB Murphy Elementary School
Chicago, IL

Harriet Carr
Holladay Elementary School
Richmond, VA

Lisa Clark
Lebanon Elementary School
Lebanon, WI

Erin Hansen
Concord Elementary School
Edina, MN

Carol Hauswald
Karel Havlicek School
Berwyn, IL

Eleanor Johnson
Weaver Lake Elementary School
Maple Grove, MN

Elma Jones
Swarthmore-Rutledge School
Swarthmore, PA

Paula Kaiser
Irving Elementary School
West Allis, WI

Amber Langerman
Jane Vernon Elementary School
Kenosha, WI

Brenda Nixon
Las Lomitas Elementary School
Atherton, CA

Pat Pagone
St. Emily School
Mt. Prospect, IL

Kelli Phillips
Maryvale Elementary School
Rockville, MD

Krista Sackett
Lawson Elementary School
Johnston, IA

Carole Skalinder
Orrington Elementary School
Evanston, IL

Dr. Karen Smith
Manoa Elementary School
Havertown, PA

Sandra Sparacino
Longfellow Elementary School
West Allis, WI

Linda Vlasic
Ormondale Elementary School
Portola Valley, CA

Dawna Work
Normandy Village Elementary
Jacksonville, FL

Student Contributors

Nicole Barbian
Longfellow Elementary School
West Allis, WI

Cara Camardella
Holladay Elementary School
Richmond, VA

Sarah Cunningham
Meadow Ridge Elementary
Orland Park, IL

Jessica Ellis
Normandy Village Elementary
Jacksonville, FL

Elizabeth Garrett
Botsford Elementary School
Livonia, MI

Charlotte Jones
Las Lomitas Elementary School
Atherton, CA

Emma Kerrigan
St. Joseph School
Wilmette, IL

Sarah Langston
Holladay Elementary School
Richmond, VA

John Lee
McKenzie Elementary School
Wilmette, IL

Sophie Lee
McKenzie Elementary School
Wilmette, IL

Nicole Naudi
Jane Vernon Elementary School
Kenosha, WI

Kate O'Donnell
Creek Valley Elementary School
Edina, MN

Tyler Peay
Pearsons Corner Elementary
School
Mechanicsville, VA

Bekka Rood
Prairieland Elementary School
Normal, IL

Caroline Ruwe
Weaver Lake Elementary School
Maple Grove, MN

Savannah Shields
Vandergriff Elementary School
Fayetteville, AR

James Thornberg
W.A. Porter Elementary School
Hurst, TX

Maria Tuite
St. Cecilia School
San Francisco, CA

Thomas R. Vanderloo
St. Jude School
Chattanooga, TN

Christian Vetter
Sacred Heart School
Lombard, IL

Jessica Walters
Karel Havlicek School
Berwyn, IL

Kiernan Ziletti
St. Bridget's Catholic School
Richmond, VA

3

Contents

2 Skills for Active Reading......44

Reader's Almanac.....392

Reading First Connections

READING FOR INFORMATION

Reading Nonfiction	Fluency, Comprehension
Focus on Nonfiction	Comprehension
Elements of Nonfiction	Vocabulary, Comprehension

READING FOR SCHOOL

Reading Textbooks	Comprehension
Focus on Textbooks	Comprehension
Elements of Textbooks	Vocabulary, Comprehension

READING STORIES AND POEMS

Reading Kinds of Literature	Fluency, Comprehension
Focus on Stories	Fluency, Comprehension
Elements of Literature	Vocabulary, Comprehension, Fluency, Phonemic Awareness

READING FOR TESTS

Reading a Test and Test Questions	Comprehension
Focus on Tests	Comprehension, Phonics

READER'S ALMANAC

Strategy Handbook	Comprehension
Reading Tools	Comprehension
Word Workshop	Phonics, Phonemic Awareness, Vocabulary

How to Use This Book

This year you will have many different assignments. You will read books and novels. You will take tests. You will start using bigger textbooks.

Now you are expected to read all of these books. So, when you get stuck, look in this handbook. It's a guide that can help you read a poem, understand a graph, or prepare a report.

Goals

This handbook has three simple goals.

1 Show You How to Read

You know how to hold a book and how to move your eyes over the page. But reading is more than that. This handbook shows what good readers do, so you'll know their secrets.

2 Teach You Reading Tools and Strategies

Part of being a good reader is knowing about reading strategies and tools. Just as a builder has different tools, so do readers.

3 Teach You about Kinds of Readings

Another goal of this handbook is to teach you about different kinds of readings. How is a folktale different from a poem? What's the difference between reading a math textbook and a science textbook? How do you read a website or a graph?

Uses for the Handbook

How can you use this handbook? Use it as a coach, a friendly parent or teacher you can turn to whenever you need help. Think of it as a guide that can lead you through the forest of readings you have to do for school. Keep it handy.

Try looking in the handbook when you do these things:

1 Homework

What happens when you have some homework and you get stuck? You may be able to answer your question by looking in the *Reader's Handbook*. It gives the meaning of all kinds of terms and information about all kinds of readings—from graphs and websites to poems and textbooks.

Try looking in the table of contents for what you need to know.

2 Reading from Textbooks

Sometime during the year you may have to read part of a textbook for homework. What do you do? First, look in the *Reader's Handbook*! It will tell you how to preview the chapter, take notes, and remember what you read.

Look in the chapter called "Reading for School" for help.

3 Book Reports

Sometime you will read a novel and need to make a book report. Where should you start? First, look in the handbook. It will tell you how to pick a good book and what to look for in the novel.

Look in the chapter called "Reading Stories and Poems" for help with novels, poems, plots, and more.

4 Reading Aloud

Have you ever been asked to read aloud? The *Reader's Handbook* will help you get ready to give an oral report or read in front of others. Look in the handbook for tips on reading aloud.

5 Tests or Quizzes

As you get older, you will start to have more tests and quizzes. How can you get ready? Look in the handbook. It tells you how to read different tests and test questions.

Look over the chapter "Reading for Tests" so you'll be ready.

Book Organization

1 Reading Lessons

For big topics like textbooks, stories, and tests, the handbook has big lessons. These lessons show you step-by-step how to use the reading process. Each reading lesson includes a checklist, a reading strategy and reading tools, and a summary that repeats the key points.

Reading a Novel

Maybe you're just beginning to read your first or second novel on your own. Or maybe you've already read many novels. Knowing how to use reading strategies and tools can help you read novels even better.

A novel is a long made-up story. Some novels have so many pages you may wonder how you can read something so long. But being longer is part of what makes novels fun. You learn much more about the characters, where they live, and what happens to them. Novels can take you into other worlds.

Goals

Here you'll learn how to:
✓ understand the characters, setting, and plot of a novel
✓ use the reading strategy of using graphic organizers

Before Reading

Before reading a novel, you should set a purpose, preview, and make a plan for reading.

282

Focus Lessons

For smaller topics like understanding characters, websites, or writing tests, the handbook has shorter lessons. These lessons are brief looks at one specific subject. Each focus lesson gives you tips, strategies, and reading tools that are just right for this kind of reading.

Focus on Characters ▉

Focus on Characters

Close your eyes and think of a story you really like. What makes it one of your favorites? One thing you probably like is the characters—the people, animals, or creatures that the story is about.

Characters are important in stories and novels. They keep the action moving, and they keep you as a reader interested. Without the characters, you wouldn't have a story!

Goals

Here you'll learn how to:
- ✔ tell the difference between major and minor characters
- ✔ find clues to help you understand characters
- ✔ see how characters change

Before Reading

From the moment you open a book, pay attention to the characters in a story. Find out who the story is about. Most stories have two kinds of characters: major and minor.

Stories and Poems

313

3 Elements Mini-lessons

For small terms or ideas, the handbook has a short mini-lesson. It explains the key terms, such as index, plot, or line graph. Each mini-lesson gives you an example, description, and definition.

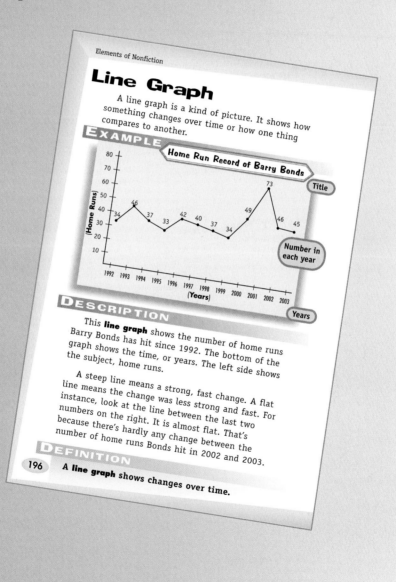

Elements of Nonfiction

Line Graph

A line graph is a kind of picture. It shows how something changes over time or how one thing compares to another.

EXAMPLE

Home Run Record of Barry Bonds

(Home Runs)

34 46 37 33 42 40 37 34 49 73 46 45

1992 1993 1994 1995 1996 1997 1998 1999 2000 2001 2002 2003
(Years)

Title

Number in each year

DESCRIPTION

Years

This **line graph** shows the number of home runs Barry Bonds has hit since 1992. The bottom of the graph shows the time, or years. The left side shows the subject, home runs.

A steep line means a strong, fast change. A flat line means the change was less strong and fast. For instance, look at the line between the last two numbers on the right. It is almost flat. That's because there's hardly any change between the number of home runs Bonds hit in 2002 and 2003.

DEFINITION

196   A **line graph** shows changes over time.

Reader's Almanac

For reading strategies and other information, check the Almanac. It's in the back of the handbook. It includes a **Strategy Handbook** and a **Reading Tools** section.

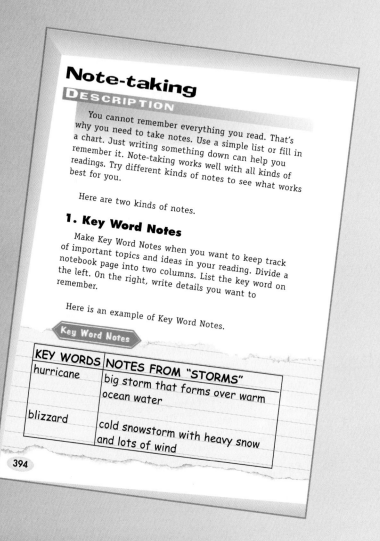

Note-taking

DESCRIPTION

You cannot remember everything you read. That's why you need to take notes. Use a simple list or fill in a chart. Just writing something down can help you remember it. Note-taking works well with all kinds of readings. Try different kinds of notes to see what works best for you.

Here are two kinds of notes.

1. Key Word Notes

Make Key Word Notes when you want to keep track of important topics and ideas in your reading. Divide a notebook page into two columns. List the key word on the left. On the right, write details you want to remember.

Here is an example of Key Word Notes.

Key Word Notes

KEY WORDS	NOTES FROM "STORMS"
hurricane	big storm that forms over warm ocean water
blizzard	cold snowstorm with heavy snow and lots of wind

394

Reader's Almanac, continued

The Reader's Almanac also includes the **Word Workshop.** It gives you information on letters and sound patterns, spelling, and prefixes and suffixes.

Letters and Sounds

Learning the sounds that letters make will help you be a better reader. You will read more smoothly, or fluently, and that will help you understand what you read better.

Short Vowels

Vowels can make different sounds. Here are examples of short vowel sounds you can hear in words.

Short a	Short e	Short i	Short o	Short u
sat	pen	hit	hot	bus
dad	sled	sit	pot	cup
lap	kept	dish	stop	sun
flag	leg	will	shop	duck
apple	best	pick	rock	club

Long Vowels

Long vowels sound similar to the letter name of the vowel. Here are examples of words with long vowel sounds. Note the way the sounds are spelled.

Long a	Long e	Long i	Long o	Long u
lake	beach	life	note	cute
hay	speed	tie	boat	glue
break	theme	high	know	juice
claim	piece	shy	most	chew
sleigh	seize	buy		(often referred to as words with oo)
	we	eye		

428

21

Introduction

- What Is Reading?
- Why Do You Read?
- What Happens When You Read

Introduction

Think about what happens when you read. You get a book. You probably sit or lie down. Then, you begin looking at words and pictures on the page. It sounds like a snap, but is it really?

No, it isn't. But you read every day! This handbook will help you develop your reading skills and muscles.

What Is Reading?

There is more to reading than you might think. Reading is a way you can learn. It can take you places you have never been, such as China or the middle of a jungle. Reading is an ability you have, like jumping rope or riding a bike. Reading is something you do that takes time, practice, and effort. Reading is thinking.

Let's look more closely at the question "What is reading?"

Reading Is a Skill

Reading is like swimming, skating, playing the drums, or pitching a softball. The more you do it, the better you get at it.

Reading Is a Tool

Reading is something you use and need. You use reading when you get an invitation. You use it to find out where you should go and what time to arrive. Reading is a tool you use with street signs, birthday cards, and homework.

Reading Is a Process

Like writing, reading is also a process. You go through a number of steps to do it. You get ready and set a goal. You read and take notes. Then, you think about what you've read and even reread parts. Each step adds something to what you learn.

Why Do You Read?

You may also sometimes wonder *why* you have to read. After all, reading can be hard at times. It takes up time when you could be out playing with your friends. So, why should you do it?

Reading Is Fun

For one thing, reading can be fun. It can be as much fun as going to the movies or watching TV. Where else do you meet interesting characters? In books, you can meet pigs that talk, mice who are heroes, and kids who are flat. Books and articles can tell you about fascinating real persons, places, and things. You can learn about Ben Franklin, the United States, and the planets.

Reading is also a way of enjoying stories. Through reading, you can enjoy bedtime stories anytime you like. You can read about princesses or superheroes, funny animals, best friends, and long-ago times.

Reading Gives You Information

Another reason you read is to learn things. You read maps to learn how to get places. A map tells you what street to take and where to turn. You read menus to decide what you want to eat. Do you want to play a new game? Read the directions.

Reading is your way to learn about the world and what's in it. By reading, you can find out about cool things like huge polar bears, super fast cars, or creepy, crawly bugs.

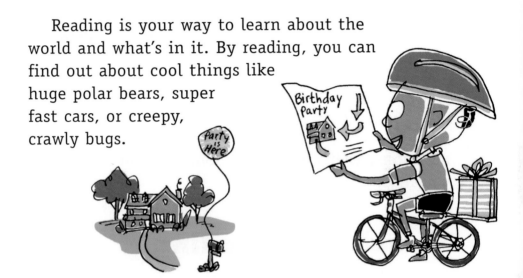

Reading Changes You

After you read a book, you aren't the same anymore. For one thing, you're a little smarter. You probably know some words you didn't know before. But you may also feel different.

After you read about a puppy without a home, you may want to get a puppy. Or, you may read about the life of a famous soccer player and want to be like him or her. Reading changes the way you think about your life, what you want to do, and who you want to be.

What Happens When You Read

Here are a few questions you should ask yourself as a reader.

What goes on in my head when I'm reading?

How would I describe reading to someone?

What does reading look like?

Right now, you may not be able to answer these questions. That's okay. Let's look at what happens when you read.

Visualizing Reading

Visualizing means you "see" something. When you visualize, you make a picture in your mind. To understand what happens when you read, do this activity.

Try these simple steps.

‹ Visualizing

1. Close your eyes. Think about a time when you were reading.

2. Picture what happened. How did you start reading?

3. Now think about what happened while you were reading. Think about where you were. Picture what was happening as you read.

4. Then think about what happened as you finished reading. What did you do then?

5. Last, draw what happens when you read.

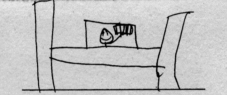

Pick up a book.
Hop in bed.

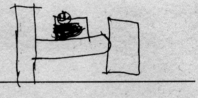

Read my book.

Put my book at
the end of my bed.

Go to sleep.

By thinking about yourself as a reader, you can become a better reader.

The Reading and Writing Process

Imagine if you were asked to jump 12 feet in the air. That would be like jumping from the ground all the way up to the second floor. That's impossible, right?

But what if you could use the stairs? Could you do it then? Yes, you probably could jump up one step at a time.

Going one step at a time makes any job easier. That's exactly what you need to do with reading. Break up what you need to do into smaller steps. Go one step at a time.

You probably already do that when you write. Well, reading and writing are both processes with several steps.

Good readers and writers know the secret that good runners know. You need to get ready and warm up. Then you need to take off. At the end, you need to stretch and relax after the race.

Let's look more closely at the processes good readers and writers use.

Writing Process

1. Prewriting

2. Drafting

3. Revising

4. Editing and Proofreading

5. Publishing

These are the main steps in writing. Writers get ready by thinking about what they will write. Then they begin writing. They stop and revise what they've written. Then they correct any mistakes. Last, they make a clean copy and publish.

Reading Process

1. **Before Reading**

2. **During Reading**

3. **After Reading**

When you read, you should also follow the same kinds of steps. The lessons in this handbook show you an easy-to-follow reading process. You can use it with all kinds of reading in school and on your own.

The next part of the handbook will tell you more about the reading process.

The Reading
Process

- Before Reading
- During Reading
- After Reading

The Reading Process

The reading process used in this handbook has three stages: Before Reading, During Reading, and After Reading. Each stage has a few steps.

Before Reading

Before you read is the "getting ready" stage. You are just starting out with a new book or article. It's like a new adventure.

When you start to read, you should do three things.

A. Set a Purpose

B. Preview

C. Plan

A Set a Purpose

You go to school to learn. You go to the library to find a book. In other words, you go places for a reason.

You read for a reason too. You might want to find out about lions or spaceships. That's your purpose for reading. You may be reading for an assignment. In that case, think about what is important to remember.

B Preview

Next, look at the reading itself. Think of this preview step as a "sneak peek." In a preview, you look ahead at what you are going to read. You want to know what to expect. Read the title and the first sentence. Think about what you may already know about the subject.

A preview doesn't take very long. Sometimes all you need is a minute or two. For a story, you might just look at the title, the first sentence, and the pictures. For an article, you might also peek at the ending. That's all you need to do to get ready to read.

Process

The end.

C Plan

The preview helps you to decide *how* you want to read. Next, you make a plan. Will you take notes? Will you visualize? Will you use graphic organizers, such as a Venn Diagram or Web?

As a reader, you have a lot of choices *how* you can read something. You don't read a poem the same way you do an article. Websites are different from tests or novels. You read different kinds of material in different ways. For each reading, come up with a reading plan. That means choosing a reading strategy. This handbook shows you six different reading strategies.

During Reading

Now you're ready. You have a purpose, an idea of what the reading is about, and a plan. Now you just read. Create pictures in your head of what the author is saying.

D. Read with a Purpose

E. Connect

D Read with a Purpose

As you read, you will learn a lot of information. You will read facts, descriptions, names, dates, and pictures. You have a lot to think about.

Active readers take charge. They make predictions and draw conclusions. They stop and check how well they understand what they're reading. They take notes or highlight important parts. They visualize as they read. You need to do that too.

Think about your reading purpose. Ask yourself, "What am I trying to learn here?" That's how you read with a purpose.

E Connect

You can become a better reader by connecting your life to what you are reading.

Think about how a book or article relates to your life and what you already know. Ask yourself questions when you read.

> **Do I already know anything about this subject?**

> **How do I feel about this?**

> **What do I think about this?**

> **How or why is this important to me?**

> **Have I seen or read something like this before?**

By asking yourself these questions, you will start to connect with the reading. As a result, you will stay interested and remember more.

Process

After Reading

What do you do when you get to the end of a book or an article? You may just close the book and put it away. But stop! You're not done reading.

The time after you finish reading the last words in a book or an article is important. Take time to collect your thoughts.

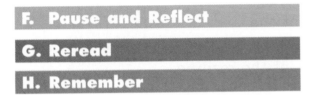

F. Pause and Reflect

G. Reread

H. Remember

F Pause and Reflect

Part of reading is thinking about what you have read. After you finish a book, stop and reflect. Ask yourself if you met your reading purpose. Did you learn everything you wanted to know? Did any part of the reading confuse you?

G Reread

Most readers,
even good ones,
need to go back
and reread a little.
In fact, some of the
best readers do the
most rereading. Few
readers learn everything in
one reading. Most of the
time you will need to look
again at some part of the reading.

Go back to the reading a second or even a third
time. That rereading can help you "fix up" your
understanding. Here are some reasons to reread:

- to learn more details about an important character
  or idea
- to look again at a part that seemed confusing
  or unclear
- to enjoy again a part that you really liked

You will have lots of reasons to reread. The most
important one is your reading purpose. Think back
about why you began reading in the first place. Did you
learn what you wanted to learn? What else do you need
or want to know?

H Remember

The last step in the reading process is to remember what you have read. The secret to remembering is to do something with the information so your brain remembers it.

How can you do that? It's easy. Here are some suggestions to try. Each one is a way to use what you learn from your reading.

- Tell a friend.
- Write an email.
- Take notes.
- Make a picture.
- Write in your Reading Notebook.

By writing or explaining something in your own words, you will make it easier to remember.

41

The Reading Process

The reading process has three main stages.

Before Reading

- Set a purpose.
- Preview the reading.
- Plan a reading strategy.

During Reading

- Read with a purpose. Look for information that fits your purpose.
- Connect your life to the reading.

Process

After Reading

■ Pause and reflect. Look back to see if you learned what you wanted to learn.

■ Read some or all of it again. Clear up anything you missed the first time.

■ Remember what you learned. Write something about it, or share it with a friend.

Skills for
Active Reading

Skills

Skills for Active Reading

What happens when you read? Do you ever feel like your eyes are going over the words, but the words aren't going into your brain? That's why you need to use your thinking skills and do active reading.

Basic Reading Skills

You predict. You make inferences. You draw conclusions. You compare. You contrast. You evaluate. Your brain never stops. You're a thinking machine! You do this every day. It's natural. And you will use these everyday thinking skills while you're reading.

Predicting

One important skill for active reading is predicting. *Predicting* means you use what you know to make a guess at what will come next. Making predictions is not hard. You have probably already done a lot of predicting.

Here's a prediction about a book.

EXAMPLES OF PREDICTING

✔ guessing if it will rain
✔ telling how you think a movie will end

Predicting

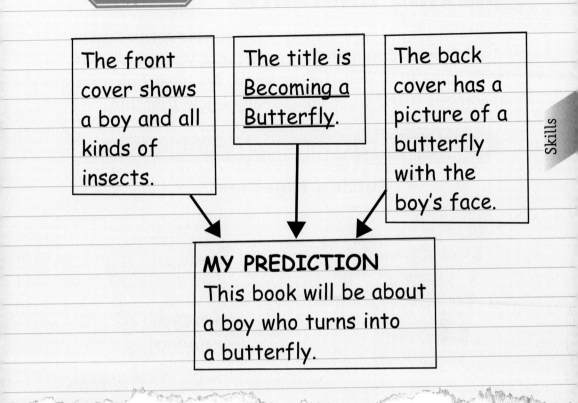

The front cover shows a boy and all kinds of insects.

The title is <u>Becoming a Butterfly</u>.

The back cover has a picture of a butterfly with the boy's face.

Skills

MY PREDICTION
This book will be about a boy who turns into a butterfly.

Active readers go back to check their predictions. It's okay if your guess turns out to be wrong. The important thing is that your brain is working. When you predict as you read, your predictions may change. That's fine. Active readers change their predictions as they get more information.

Making Inferences

Making inferences is another skill for active reading. An *inference* puts together something you see or read with something you already know. An important part of reading is using what you already know from life.

A Plan for Making Inferences

Putting together

what you know

+

what you learn from reading

GOOD READER

You make inferences every day. You figure out that your friend is angry when you see him frown and slam the door. You figure out a storm is coming when dark clouds gather in the sky and you hear thunder.

Let's look at another example. One morning your friend coughs and sneezes a lot. What inference can you make?

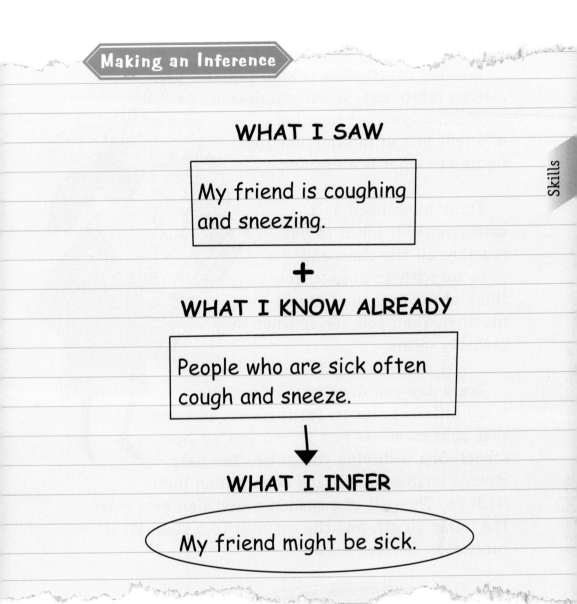

Making an Inference

WHAT I SAW

My friend is coughing and sneezing.

+

WHAT I KNOW ALREADY

People who are sick often cough and sneeze.

↓

WHAT I INFER

My friend might be sick.

Skills

You need to make inferences while you're reading. It will often be up to you to figure out what's happening, how a character feels, or what a sentence means. Writers won't always tell you everything. Remember to put together the words on the page with what you already know about the subject.

Drawing Conclusions

Drawing conclusions is kind of like making inferences. When you draw a conclusion, you put together different bits of information and figure out what it all means.

Think of yourself as a detective. Your job is to put together all the clues and come up with an answer. You think about how the facts fit together. Then you decide what they probably mean.

Every day you draw conclusions about many different things. For instance, imagine that your mom has just picked you up from school. She is driving you home. You hear strange engine sounds and see warning lights flash on. Then all of a sudden everything gets quiet. The lights go off, and the car rolls to a stop. What conclusion can you draw?

Drawing a Conclusion

FACT 1

The car makes a strange noise as we are driving home.

+

FACT 2

The engine warning lights go on.

+

FACT 3

The lights go off, and the car rolls to a stop.

↓

CONCLUSION

Something is wrong with the car.

Skills

Drawing conclusions works the same way during reading as it does in real life. As you read, pay attention to facts and details. Think about how one event or idea connects to another. Drawing conclusions helps put the pieces together and lets you look at the whole picture.

Comparing and Contrasting

Another basic thinking skill is comparing and contrasting. When you compare and contrast two things, you think about how they are alike and how they are different. This helps you understand both things a little better.

By now, you have probably done lots of comparing and contrasting. Have you noticed who is tallest in your class and who is shortest? Can you give examples of how you and your sister or brother are alike and how you are different? You know these things because you compare and contrast every day.

Look at this example. How are the two jackets alike and different?

Comparing and Contrasting

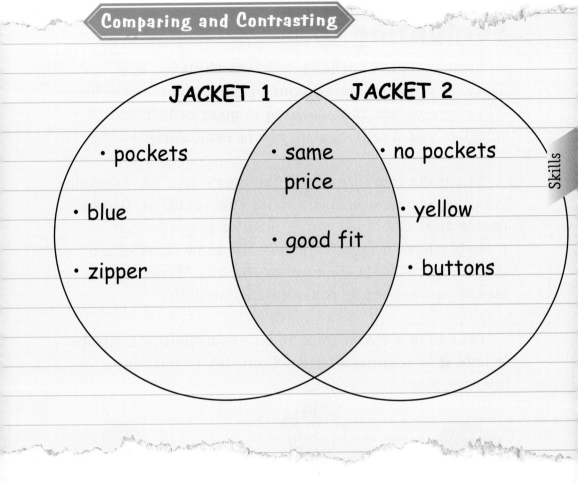

Skills

Which jacket would you buy? Which one you want depends on whether you like yellow or blue and want buttons or pockets. You compare and contrast these two jackets before you make a choice.

As a reader, look for similarities and differences. Even if the author does not tell you directly, you can usually see them. Get in the habit of comparing and contrasting the characters, settings, events, and ideas as you read.

Evaluating

Evaluating is another important thinking skill. *Evaluating* means giving your opinion about something. When you decide if something is good or bad and whether you like it or not, you're evaluating.

You make lots of evaluations every day. For example, you like one kind of pasta more than another. Or you decide that the book you're reading is good. You probably have a favorite movie, TV show, kind of ice cream, sports team, or teacher. Having "favorites" means you are using your evaluation skills.

Let's take a closer look at an evaluation of a coach. It lists four reasons why Mr. Gonzalez is someone's favorite coach.

Evaluating

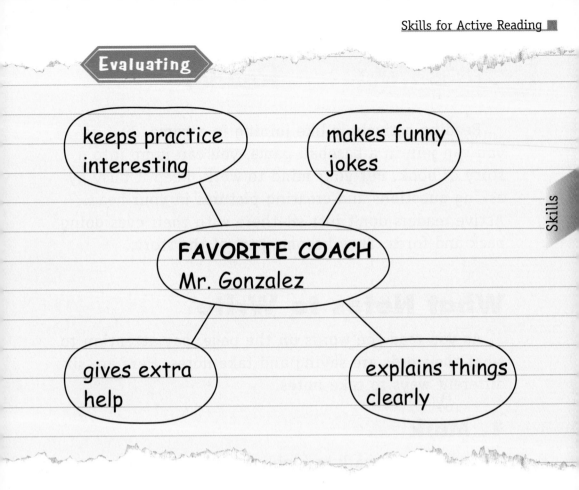

keeps practice interesting

makes funny jokes

FAVORITE COACH
Mr. Gonzalez

gives extra help

explains things clearly

You also make evaluations as you read. For instance, when you read a story, you decide whether or not you like the characters. What you decide depends a lot on your beliefs and experiences. Of course, it also depends on what the characters say and do.

You like to read books on some subjects but not others. You might like books on horses but not spiders. As a reader, ask yourself, "What do I think about this? What reasons support my opinion?" Then make your evaluation. That's being an active reader and using your brain.

Being an Active Reader

Reading actively is like joining in a game. Just as you can join in a baseball game, you can jump into a story or book. Put your mind to work. Keep it busy by asking questions and creating pictures in your head. Active readers don't just sit there with their eyes going back and forth. They become part of the story.

What Notes to Write

As you read the words on the page, pay attention to what the words are saying and take notes. Here are six different ways to take notes.

1. Mark

As you read, mark or highlight key words and sentences. Circle or underline ones that seem important to you. If the book does not belong to you, you'll have to use other paper or sticky notes. Look at how one reader marked important parts of these sentences.

> **from *Tornado* by Betsy Byars**
>
> At breakfast that morning, I remember my mother looked up from the stove, took a breath, and said, "I smell a storm."
> I shivered a little, because my mother's nose was always right.

A storm is coming.

2. React

While you're reading, react to what the words are saying. Remember, the author is trying to tell you something. You can react the same way you would react to a friend who's talking to you. Here is an example.

from *Tornado*

My daddy said, "Well, you kids better stay close to the house."

The morning went by, slow and scary. We did stay close to the house. Folks didn't call our part of the country *Tornado Alley* for nothing.

Along about lunch, it hit. Only there was no warning like we had today. No funnel cloud, no nothing. One minute we were eating beans and biscuits at the table. Next there was a roar—worse than a train—worse than a hundred trains. And then there came a terrible tearing sound, like the world was being ripped apart. I can still hear it in my mind.

> My dad would say the same thing.

> That would scare me!

3. Ask Questions

While you're reading, ask yourself questions. Is the meaning clear? Are you wondering about something? Ask questions just as though the author were there to answer you. Here are some example questions.

from *Tornado*

I looked up, and I saw sky. The ceiling was clean gone. There was the sky! The tornado had torn the roof off the kitchen and left the food on the table and us in our seats.

My daddy was the first to be able to speak. He said, "Well, I'm surprised to find myself alive."

That was how we all felt. We looked at our arms and legs to make sure they were still hooked on us.

Then my father pushed back his chair and said, "Let's go see the damage."

How long did the tornado last?

What will they see?

4. Create Pictures

Try to create pictures in your head as you read descriptions in a story or book. Try to *picture* what the author wants you to see. As you read, draw what you see in your head. By drawing, you will understand and remember more of what you read. Here's what one reader "saw" while reading.

from *Tornado*

Outside, the yard was not our yard anymore. The tree with the tire swing was laid flat. The tops of all the pine trees had been snapped off. A doghouse I had never seen before was beside the well. A piece of bicycle was here, the hood of a car there. I stepped over somebody's clothesline that still had some clothes on it.

The roof of the kitchen lay at the edge of the garden. It was folded shut like a book. We walked over there.

5. Make Things Clear

As you read, make sure that things are clear to you. If you don't quite understand what the author is saying, try to figure it out. Every page or so, write down what you've understood so far. Look at how these notes help to make things clear.

from *Tornado*

"It was about time for a new roof," my daddy said. He always tried to find the good in something.

I was just walking around, looking at other people's things, when I heard a rattling noise.

> He wants to know what the noise is.

I kept listening and looking, and finally I realized the sound was coming from that doghouse. I went over to it.

The doghouse was trembling. You could see it. It was trembling. It was shaking. It was doing everything but having a fit.

I looked inside, and there was a big black dog. He was panting so hard, I could feel his breath. He was shaking so hard, the doghouse was in danger of losing its boards.

> The dog is really scared.

6. Predict

As you read, try to predict what will happen next. Think ahead when you read. Use what you are learning from the story to make a guess, or prediction, about what will happen. Here's an example.

from *Tornado*

"Daddy, there's a dog in here!"
My daddy came over.
"Look, Daddy. It's a big black dog."
My daddy leaned down and took a look.
"Well, you can come on out now," he told the dog. "The storm's over, and you're among friends."
The dog just kept shaking.
"Maybe I can pull him out," I said.
"Don't you put your hand in there," my mother said.
"Yes, leave him be, Pete."

I think the dog will come out soon.

I predict Pete will want to keep the dog.

Making predictions helps you stay interested and involved in what you're reading.

Where to Write Notes

When you read actively, you need a pencil and paper. As you read, write down your reactions, questions, and predictions. Draw the pictures you create in your mind. Here are some ways to do that.

Use Sticky Notes

If a book *doesn't* belong to you, you can't write in it. But you can always use sticky notes. Here's an example of how one active reader used sticky notes.

from *Tornado*

All that day, all that night, all the next day that dog shook. I brought him water, but he wouldn't drink. I brought him food, but he wouldn't eat.

Write on the Page

When the book *does* belong to you, you can mark important sentences and words right on the page. You can also write notes in the margins. Here's an example.

from *Tornado*

Then that night my mother leaned out the kitchen door and yelled, "Supper!" as she usually did. The dog heard her and stuck his head out of the doghouse. He must have been familiar with the word.

The dog comes out!

Write in a Notebook

Sometimes you may want to write notes about what you read in a special notebook. You can also use a separate piece of paper or a note card. Just be sure you write down the title and the page number.

> **from *Tornado***
>
> He came out, stood there, looked around for a moment, and then gave one final shake, as if he were shaking off the past. Then he came over and joined us at the back door.
>
> I said, "Daddy, can we keep him? Please?"
>
> "If we don't find the owner."
>
> "Can we call him Tornado?"
>
> "Until we find the owner."
>
> "We'll have to ask around," my mother reminded me.
>
> "I know."

Name of the dog

Tornado Notes

p. 2   They decide to call the dog Tornado.

Ways to Be a Good Reader

You can see people reading at many times and in many places. They read while riding on a bus or train. They read sitting in the doctor's office or waiting for a ride home from school. Some people even read while they're walking down the street!

Find a Reading Place

Even though you can read anywhere, having a special place to read can help you read better. A good reading place is quiet and comfortable. You're alone. The TV isn't on. No one is talking to you or walking by you. A big chair in the corner of a room may be just perfect.

If you don't have a place like that, it's okay. You can create a comfy corner with pillows and blankets. Let your family know that's your special reading place. Ask them to try to be quiet around it when you go there to read.

WHAT A GOOD READING PLACE HAS

- ✔ good light
- ✔ peace and quiet
- ✔ comfortable chair
- ✔ pen, pencil, or highlighter
- ✔ sticky notes or a notebook

Find Time for Reading

Reading each day is one of the most important things you can do. This means finding time to read for fun. This kind of reading is not the reading you have to do for school. This is reading just for you. You could read books by your favorite author, a magazine, a joke book, or books of amazing facts.

You should read for fun 20 to 40 minutes every day or almost every day. Sometimes it's hard to find that much extra time. But reading for fun every day is the best thing you can do to be a good student. Reading takes practice. The more you practice, the better you'll be at it.

So, make a plan. Read at the same time every day. Some people like to read in bed each night before they go to sleep. Some people like to read when they get home from school or right after dinner. Make reading a daily habit for you.

Baseball 4:00

Reading 5:00

Dinner 5:30

Skills

Choose a Good Book

How can you know if a book will be good? How do you know if it will be too easy or too hard? Choosing a book that is good for you is a skill you need to learn.

What's in a Book?

When you pick up a book, you probably look at its cover. Too often readers grab any old book just because of what's on the cover or because of its subject. There's more to it than that. Here are some other things to consider.

Choosing a Book

What It Looks Like
- size of the print
- number of pages
- pictures or drawings

What It's About
- topic or subject
- kind of book (novel, biography, poetry)
- your interest in the topic

How It's Written
- long or hard words
- lots of long sentences

Howdy partner!

Try the Five Finger Test to tell if the book is too hard. Put one finger down each time you don't know a word. If all five go down on one page, the book may be too hard to enjoy reading on your own.

Previewing a Book

When you go to the library, you probably have some ideas about what kinds of books you like. Here are some tips for choosing a good book.

- Make a list of three or four things that interest you.
- Ask some friends what books or authors they like.
- Keep a list of subjects you'd like to learn about.
- Ask your teacher or the librarian for book ideas.

Now you are ready to start searching. Use the computer catalog. Look for books on a particular subject or by a particular author. Next, find those books on the library shelves. Collect three to six different books. Take them to a table, sit down, and start to go through them.

Here's a quick, easy way to sample the books, form an opinion about them, and pick the best ones for you.

Skills

How to Preview a Book

1. Look at the front and back cover.
- What is the book about?
- How interesting does it look?

2. Look at the first page or two.
- How does the book start?
- What's the writing like?
- Are the words easy or hard to read?

3. Look at the table of contents.
- What do the chapter titles tell you?
- How is it organized?

4. Flip through the pages.
- How long is the book?
- What do the pages look like?

How to Read Aloud

Besides choosing a good book, you also need to learn how to read a book aloud. Most of the time you will sit by yourself and read silently. But at some point you will be asked to read aloud.

Why Read Aloud?

Part of the fun of reading is sharing what you learn. You share other good times, like movies with friends, so why not reading? You learn when people read to you and when you read to them.

Here are some fun ways to read aloud with friends or classmates.

Reading Aloud

Read with a buddy.
Read one paragraph. Then ask a buddy to read the next. Go back and forth.

Perform a reading.
Form a group with three or four friends and read in front of the class. Be sure to mark the part you will read. Read it aloud several times before you get up in front of the class.

Record what you read.
Get a tape recorder. Find a part of a book you like. Practice reading that part of the book aloud. Then turn the tape recorder on and record yourself reading.

Tips for Reading Aloud

What do good readers do when they read aloud? They read with expression in a clear and accurate way without mistakes. They are smooth and even in the way they read. And, they hold your interest. Here are three tips.

1. Be Clear and Accurate

■ Read without skipping or stumbling over words.

■ Read loudly and clearly.

■ Pronounce the words carefully.

Say _gov•ern•ment._

2. Read Smoothly

■ Read with a rhythm.

■ Go faster or slower as needed.

■ Read without saying "ah" or "um."

■ Use commas and periods to tell you when to pause.

■ Think how words go together in groups.

Sitting alone in his room, the boy smiled.

3. Be Interesting

■ Read with feeling. If a character is sad, sound sad.

■ Change the tone and pitch of your voice.

■ Stress important words.

The police officer yelled, "STOP!"

How to Prepare

What's the secret of reading aloud? One secret is to practice. Everyone needs to prepare. First, always read silently before reading aloud. Look up any words that you don't understand. Remember to practice looking at your audience from time to time. And, practice reading the sentences clearly and smoothly.

HOW TO PREPARE FOR READING ALOUD

✔ practice
✔ practice
✔ practice

Ask a friend or family member to listen as you read aloud. Ask them for suggestions. Read to them a couple of times. Do it differently each time. For instance, read some sentences super slowly or say some words in a quiet whisper. Then ask them which way they prefer.

Summing Up

- As an active reader, you use these basic reading skills all of the time:
  - predicting
  - making inferences
  - drawing conclusions
  - comparing and contrasting
  - evaluating
- Write notes, ask questions, and make pictures as you read.
- Write on sticky notes, the page itself, or in a special notebook.
- Find a quiet reading place, and make time to read for fun every day.
- To choose a good book, preview what it's about and how it's written.
- To read aloud well, read clearly and smoothly. Change the tone and pitch of your voice.

Words and Their Meaning

- Understanding Letters and Sounds
- Understanding Words and Word Parts
- Learning New Words
- Using a Dictionary
- Using Context Clues
- Answering Vocabulary Questions

Words

Words and Their **Meaning**

We need words! We use words all the time to express what we want to say. What makes up words?

Letters, sounds, and syllables are the building blocks of words. You put sounds together, like you put blocks together, to make something bigger—something different.

Understanding Letters and Sounds

You probably learned the letters of the alphabet a long time ago. You also know that the letters stand for different sounds. Letters can be put together in different ways to make thousands of words.

Letters

The English alphabet has 26 letters. There are 21 consonants and 5 vowels. Sometimes the letter *y* is a vowel, too. All English words have at least one vowel.

Letters can be either uppercase or lowercase. Uppercase means a capital letter (*F*), and lowercase means a small letter (*f*). The Alphabet Chart on the next page shows all of the different uppercase and lowercase letters.

Alphabet Chart

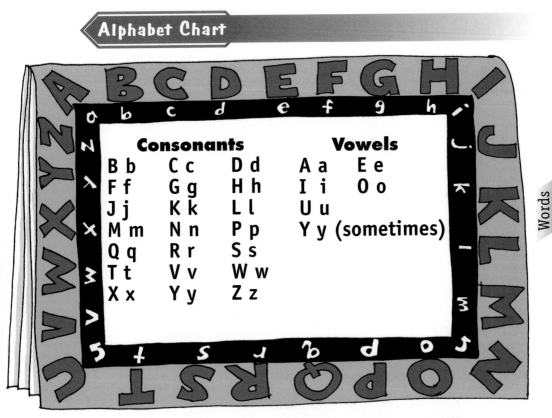

Consonants			Vowels	
B b	C c	D d	A a	E e
F f	G g	H h	I i	O o
J j	K k	L l	U u	
M m	N n	P p	Y y (sometimes)	
Q q	R r	S s		
T t	V v	W w		
X x	Y y	Z z		

How Letters Make Sounds

The problem with English is that some letters make more than one sound. Also, in English, two or more letters can work together to make just one sound.

Most of the consonants only have one sound, no matter what word they're in. For instance, *m* has the same sound in *mat, hammer,* and *gum.* But some consonants have a few different sounds. The letter *c* has one sound in *cat* but a different sound in *cent.*

Look at the chart of consonant sounds and spellings on the next page.

Sound	Spellings of Sound		
b	bat	rubbing	
d	dance	puddle	
f	fast	phone	rough
g	gum	good	
h	hat	who	
j	jump	gym	
k	cat	kick	
l	lake	tall	needle
m	man	thumb	
n	no	sudden	
p	pop	happy	
r	right	rhyme	
s	sat	miss	scene
t	tag	stopped	
v	van	cave	
w	wolf	with	
z	zero	rose	size

Vowel sounds have even more different spellings than consonant sounds. Most vowels have two main sounds—long and short. For example, the word *cape* has a **long a** sound, and *cap* has a **short a** sound.

Look at the next chart that shows the different ways some simple vowel sounds are spelled.

Vowel Sounds

Letter	Short vowel	Long vowel				
a	pat	cape	maid	pay		
e	met	be	bee	meat	easy	piano
i	hit	hike	pie	by	high	
o	top	go	toad	row	toe	
u	rug					

Some other letters go together to make completely new sounds. Think of the **ch** in *chicken* or *change* and the **oy** in *boy* or *toy*. Does this sound confusing? Don't worry. The more you practice reading, the better you'll get at knowing which sounds go with which letters. Soon you'll know them without thinking.

See the Almanac on pages 428–432 for more help with the sounds different letters make.

Sounds and Syllables

Knowing how to break hard and long words into syllables can help you be a better reader and speller.

Sounds and Spelling

There are 44 different sounds in the English language. Just as some letters have more than one sound, some sounds can be spelled in several different ways. Here are six ways to spell the **long a** sound.

Spellings of Long *a*

same	play	hey
wait	break	weigh

Now think of the sound that the letter **s** makes. In some words, the **s** sound is shown by **s**, as in sun. But, in other words, the **s** sound is spelled by **c**, as in circle.

You probably already know most of the simple vowel and consonant sounds. But do you know about the less common ones? For example, look at these sounds.

Less Common Sounds

Consonant Sounds			Vowel Sounds		
ch	church	hitch	ä	card	father
wh	where	which	oi	boy	noise
kw	choir	quick	ə	ago	pencil

See the Almanac on pages 433–437 for help with spelling.

Syllables

A *syllable* is each part of a word with a vowel sound. A word has as many syllables as it has vowel sounds. Look at the examples below. Read each word out loud. Then clap your hands softly each time you hear a new vowel sound. For example, for **break • fast**, you would clap twice.

Syllable Chart

One-syllable Words
dog
plant
make

Two-syllable Words
din • ner
flow • er
gi • ant

Three-syllable Words
Sat • ur • day
dan • ger • ous
im • por • tant

Four-syllable Words
tel • e • vi • sion
in • ter • est • ing
un • u• su • al

Five-syllable Words
ex • am • i • na • tion
un • be • liev • a • ble
dis • a • bil • i • ty

Six-syllable Words
un • nec • es • sar • i • ly
ir • reg • u • lar • i • ty
im • prob • a • bil • i • ty

Figuring Out Big Words

What do you do when you're reading and come to a really long word? How do you figure out what it is? You can use what you know about letters, sounds, and syllables to figure out those big words. Look at this example.

The Olympic games are an <u>international</u> sports event.

How do you say and understand a long word like *international*? Here is a plan you can use when you come to big words you don't know.

1. Look for Little Words and Sounds

Start at the beginning and break the big word into parts. Look for little words, or *chunks,* that you can say. Can you see *in*? Divide the big word into syllables. Then, say the whole word, one chunk at a time. You might say this: *in • ter • na • tion • al.*

2. Look for Parts You Know

Next, try to put together some of the chunks. Do you see or hear anything that looks familiar?

inter • nation • al

Inter may remind you of *Internet*. You may also see the word *nation*—another word for "country." Maybe you've seen *al* in other words. The more you read, the better you'll become at sounding out parts of big words.

3. Put It All Together

Because of *nation,* maybe you know *international* has something to do with a country or countries. Think about other words with *inter*—*interrupt* or *interfere. Inter* means "between or among."

Go back to how the word is used in the sentence. *The Olympic games are an <u>international</u> sports event.* Now the sentence makes more sense. *International* means "between nations." Countries from all over the world compete in the Olympics.

Words

Understanding Words and Word Parts

Sounding out a word and breaking it into syllables can help you make sense of a new word. Also, try learning about these kinds of words and word parts.

Kinds of Words and Word Parts

TYPE	EXAMPLE
prefixes	in, non, un
suffixes	ly, ness, ize
roots	luna, dic, scrib
homophones	to, too, two
confusing pairs	then, than

Paying attention to words and word parts is a good way to build a great vocabulary. For example, let's say you come across a hard word.

Alex was too <u>irresponsible</u> to have a dog.

How could you figure out what *irresponsible* means? Start by sounding it out.

ir • re • spon • si • ble or **ir • respons • ible**

You may think *respons* looks like *respond*. That may give you some idea of the word's meaning. But, if you knew that *ir* is a common prefix, you'd know even more. The prefix *ir* means "not." So *irresponsible* means "not responsible," or "not able to be trusted."

Prefixes, Suffixes, and Roots

Try to learn about three kinds of word parts.

1. Prefixes

2. Suffixes

3. Roots

Prefixes

A *prefix* is a word part added to the beginning of a word. A prefix changes the meaning of a word. Knowing what different prefixes mean will help you figure out new words. Here are some helpful prefixes to know.

Prefixes

Prefix	Meaning	Example
anti	against	antiwar—against war
inter	between	interview—conversation between two people
pre	before	prepay—pay money ahead of time
under	below	underwater—below the water

Many prefixes mean "not" or "opposite of."

dis	disagree—not agree with
il	illegal—not legal
in	incorrect—not correct
non	nonsense—something that doesn't make sense

See page 438 to learn more about prefixes.

Suffixes

A *suffix* is a word part that comes at the end of a word. A suffix changes the form of a word and often what part of speech it is.

Kinds of Suffixes

Suffixes That Make Nouns	Meaning	Example
ist	a person who	novelist
ment	act of	amusement
sion	state of	tension

Suffixes That Make Verb Forms	Meaning	Example
ed	past tense	talked
ize	to become	familiarize
en	to cause to	brighten

Suffixes That Make Adjectives	Meaning	Example
able	can do	readable
est	most	tallest
ful	full of	hopeful
less	without	fearless

See page 439 to learn more about suffixes.

Roots

A *root* is the main part of a word. Knowing even just a few word roots will help you figure out the meaning of lots of words.

Kinds of Roots

Root	Meaning	Examples
div	separate	divide, division
gram	write	grammar, telegram
magn, mega	big	magnificent, megaphone
mem	remember	memory, memo
multi	many	multimedia, multicultural
port	carry	transport, import
tele	far	telescope, telephone
therm	heat	thermos, thermometer

tele-phone

tele = far

Homophones

Homophones can be confusing. They are words that sound exactly alike, but they are spelled differently and mean different things. When you're reading, the other words in the sentence will help you figure out which meaning is the right one. Here are some common homophones.

Common Homophones

ant	An ant is an insect.
aunt	My aunt lives in Tennessee.
ate	Lisa ate the cake.
eight	Juan has eight fish.
buy	She wanted to buy the bike.
by	We drove by your house.
cent	The candy cost only one cent.
sent	Grandma sent us a present.
scent	The perfume has a sweet scent.
for	I got a bike for my birthday.
four	My dad has four blue shirts.
here	I'm glad you came here.
hear	He couldn't hear what she said.
it's	When it's noon, we will leave.
its	The puppy hurt its paw.

Common Homophones, continued

hole	There's a hole in my sock.
whole	She ate the whole pizza!
knew	He knew the answers on the test.
new	She has a new soccer ball.
read	Yesterday I read my book.
red	I like my red shirt.
right	All her math homework was right.
write	Did you write your name on your paper?
their	Do you like their shoes?
there	I put the book over there.
they're	They're coming to the party.
threw	He threw the ball across the street.
through	Her dad drove through the tunnel.
to	Zack went to the museum.
too	I wanted to go too.
two	We saw two baby pandas.
wait	Please wait for me by the door.
weight	The nurse wrote down my weight.
weak	The little puppy was weak.
week	Next week is my piano lesson.
your	I like your hair.
you're	You're the best speller I know!

Words

Confusing Word Pairs

Homophones can be confusing because they are words that sound alike. Other word pairs are confusing because they sound almost alike or they're spelled almost the same.

Here are some confusing word pairs and how they're used. Look out for them as you read.

Confusing Word Pairs

accept	Will you accept this gift? (*Accept* means "to receive.")
except	Everyone went except me. (*Except* means "other than.")
advice	My grandma gave me good advice.
advise	Will you advise me about what to do?
affect	Heat does not affect me.
effect	The effect of the rain was a flood.
angel	The angel costume was pretty.
angle	We measured an angle in math class.
capital	The capital of Illinois is Springfield.
capitol	Our capitol building is huge.
chose	He chose a good movie. (*Chose* is past tense of *choose*.)
choose	I choose to play the violin. (*Choose* is present tense.)

Confusing Word Pairs, continued

desert	The desert is a hot, sandy place.
dessert	She wanted cake for dessert.
lay	He will lay the blanket on the bed.
lie	We will lie down and rest soon.
loose	The button on her coat is loose.
lose	Don't lose your lunch box today!
metal	The car is made of metal.
medal	He won a medal in the Olympics.
quiet	People should be quiet in the library.
quite	She was quite a good dancer.
quit	He wanted to quit studying.
sit	She will sit in the back seat.
set	Lauren set the table last night.
than	I'm older than she is.
then	Brad will go to the pet store first and then to the grocery store.
though	We will come, though we'll be late.
through	The highway goes through town.
trail	Did you walk along the trail?
trial	The robbers will go on trial tomorrow.
weather	The weather is cloudy and cool.
whether	Do you know whether the Cubs won?
were	Were you finished with dinner?
where	Where did you put my coat?

Words

Learning New Words

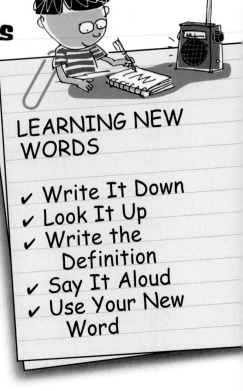

You can see and hear new words almost anywhere. You hear them in a conversation or on TV. You see them in books or on signs. But seeing or hearing them once isn't the same as really learning them. You have to work a little harder to learn them and remember them.

Here is a five-step plan for learning a new word.

LEARNING NEW WORDS

✔ Write It Down
✔ Look It Up
✔ Write the Definition
✔ Say It Aloud
✔ Use Your New Word

1. Write It Down

When you read or hear a word you don't know, write it down in a special notebook. You can also jot down where it came from.

Word Notebook

English Class—May 4
from <u>The Kid in the Red Jacket</u>

<u>fidgeting</u>, p. 7

<u>emotions</u>, p. 8

2. Look It Up

When you see or hear a word you don't know, you can always ask someone what it means. But sometimes no one else is around. Sometimes the person you ask isn't sure what the word means either.

Then you need to look up the word in a dictionary. When you look up *fidgeting*, remember to drop the *ing* and search for *fidget*—the main form of the word.

Words

from *The American Heritage Children's Dictionary*

fidget *verb* To move in a nervous or restless way: *I fidgeted in my seat while waiting to give my presentation to the class.*
fidg•et (fĭj´ĭt) *verb* **fidgeted, fidgeting**

Now you know the meaning of this word. Look at the example sentence given in the definition. Does the example help you understand the word better?

91

3. Write the Definition

Now write the definition down in your notebook. You don't have to write the definition *exactly* as it is in the dictionary. In fact, it's a good idea to put the definition into your own words. That will help you understand it and remember it. Check to be sure your own words make sense.

Word Notebook

English Class—May 4
from <u>The Kid in the Red Jacket</u>

<u>fidgeting</u>, p. 7—moving around nervously

<u>emotions</u>, p. 8

4. Say It Aloud

Now say the word and the definition out loud. This will help you remember it better.

Some words don't sound the way they look. For example, *fidget* is not pronounced *fid • get*. If you aren't sure how to pronounce the word, look back at how it's written in the dictionary. Ask a teacher or a friend to help you. *Fidget* is written as "**fĭj'**ĭt"—that's how you pronounce it. The **g** in *fidget* makes the **soft j** sound, as in *fudge* or *gadget*. Say the part that's in boldface with more stress.

5. Use Your New Word

To make the new word your own, use it when you're talking or writing. The more you use a new word, the faster it will become part of your vocabulary.

■ Find a way to use the word right away. For example, you might describe all the kids *fidgeting* at their desks.

■ Ask your little brother or sister to stop *fidgeting* during dinner.

■ Tell your teacher you're sorry for *fidgeting* during class.

Words

93

A runner needs to exercise his or her muscles, right? Well, you need to exercise your new word skills too. Here are some fun ways to do that.

Read.
The number one thing you can do to improve your vocabulary is to read. So read, read, read—read anything you want.

Learn a word a day.
Look for a new word to learn every day. Write it down in your Word Notebook. Then, when you have time, find out its meaning, and write it down.

Search for synonyms or antonyms.
Look for words that mean the same as a word you already know. Or, find words that mean the opposite. Add them to your Word Notebook.

Hunt for homophones.
Watch out for homophones. Write a sentence for each of them to help you keep track of their different meanings.

Collect interesting words.
Some words are interesting or fun, like *level*. It's spelled the same forward and backward. Other words sound or look weird, like *yak* or *llama*.

Play word games.
Word games are fun and build your vocabulary at the same time. Try doing a crossword puzzle.

Using a Dictionary

Everyone needs to learn how to use a dictionary. Sometimes you may not feel like looking up a word, because it seems like it takes too long. But the more you use a dictionary, the faster you get. And the more words you know, the better reader you'll be! Keep a dictionary nearby when you read.

Why to Use a Dictionary

Use a dictionary to find out many things:

- what a word means
- how to spell a word
- how to pronounce a word
- how to split a word into syllables

Features

Dictionaries have many parts, or features. Here are some of the more useful ones. Look for them on the sample dictionary page.

Features of a Dictionary

1. Guide Words

These are words at the very top of the page. They tell you what the first and last words on that page are. Guide words help you find the words you're looking for.

2. Entry Words

These are the words being defined. They're listed in alphabetical order and usually shown in bold.

3. Definitions

These are the phrases after the entry word. They tell you what the entry word means. Some words have two or more different meanings.

4. Sample Sentence

This is a sentence that shows you an example of how the word can be used.

5. Part of Speech

This tells you whether a word is a noun, verb, adjective, adverb, pronoun, or another type of word. This also helps you understand how the word is used.

1. Guide words

from *The American Heritage Children's Dictionary*

clank ▶ classroom

2. Entry word

clank *noun* A loud sound like that of two pieces of heavy metal hitting together: *The iron gate closed with a clank.* ◊ *verb* To make or cause to make such a sound.
clank (klăngk) ◊ *noun, plural* **clanks** ◊ *verb* **clanked, clanking**

clap *verb* **1.** To strike the hands together noisily and quickly: *The teacher clapped to get the class's attention.* **2.** To strike the hands together to show approval: *We clapped at the end of the play.* **3.** To slap with the open hand in a friendly way: *I clapped my friend on the shoulder when we met.* ◊ *noun* **1.** The loud sound of thunder. **2.** A friendly slap with the open hand.
clap (klăp) ◊ *verb* **clapped, clapping** ◊ *noun, plural* **claps**

3. Definition

clapper *noun* The part in a bell that hits the side of the bell and makes it ring.
clap·per (klăp′ər) ◊ *noun, plural* **clappers**

clarify *verb* To make easier to understand by explaining: *The coach clarified the rules of the game for us.*
clar·i·fy (klăr′ə fī′) ◊ *verb* **clarified, clarifying**

clarinet *noun* A musical instrument that has a long tube-shaped body. A clarinet is played by blowing into the mouthpiece while covering holes in the tube with the fingers or keys in order to change pitch.
clar·i·net (klăr′ə **nĕt′**) ◊ *noun, plural* **clarinets**

clarity *noun* The condition or quality of being clear.
clar·i·ty (klăr′ĭ tē) ◊ *noun*

4. Sample sentence

clash *verb* **1.** To make or strike together with a loud, harsh noise, as of two heavy metal objects striking together: *The drums boomed and the cymbals clashed.* **2.** To be against one another; disagree: *The candidates clashed during the debate.* ◊ *noun* **1.** A loud, harsh sound. **2.** A strong disagreement.
clash (klăsh) ◊ *verb* **clashed, clashing** ◊ *noun, plural* **clashes**

clasp *noun* **1.** Something, as a hook or buckle, used to hold two things together. **2.** A strong grasp or hold: *I held the railing with a*

■ clarinet

firm clasp. ◊ *verb* **1.** To fasten with or as if with a clasp. **2.** To hold or take hold of the hand or the arms: *We clasped hands when we met.*
clasp (klăsp) ◊ *noun, plural* **clasps** ◊ *verb* **clasped, clasping**

class *noun* **1.** A group of things or persons that are alike in some way; kind: *There is a very large class of sports in which a ball is used.* **2.** A group of persons who earn about the same amount and live in a similar way. **3.** A group of students learning together at a regularly scheduled time: *My class is a good group of kids.* **4.** The time during which such a class meets, or the meeting of the class: *No talking is allowed during class.* **5.** A rank or division in terms of such things as quality: *We always travel first class.* ◊ *verb* To place in a group of similar objects or persons; classify: *This book can be classed as a mystery.*
class (klăs) ◊ *noun, plural* **classes** ◊ *verb* **classed, classing**

classic *adjective* **1.** Being the very best. **2.** Being a model or standard. ◊ *noun* **1.** An artist, writer, or work of the best kind: *"Treasure Island" is a classic.* **2. classics** The literature of ancient Greece and Rome.
clas·sic (klăs′ĭk) ◊ *adjective* ◊ *noun, plural* **classics**

classical *adjective* **1.** Of or relating to the art, literature, and way of life of ancient Greece and Rome. **2.** Of or relating to music that is composed according to certain forms that have grown up over a long period of time in Europe. Operas and symphonies are examples of classical music.
clas·si·cal (klăs′ĭ kəl) ◊ *adjective*

classification *noun* **1.** The act of classifying. **2.** The system that results from classifying.
clas·si·fi·ca·tion (klăs′ə fĭ kā′shən) ◊ *noun, plural* **classifications**

classify *verb* To put into groups or classes; sort: *The librarian classified the new books.*
clas·si·fy (klăs′ə fī′) ◊ *verb* **classified, classifying**

classmate *noun* A member of the same class in school.
class·mate (klăs′māt′) ◊ *noun, plural* **classmates**

classroom *noun* A room in which classes meet in school.
class·room (klăs′rōōm′ *or* klăs′rŏŏm′) ◊ *noun, plural* **classrooms**

5. Part of speech

Words

Using Context Clues

You might not need or want to look up every word you don't know. Be a detective when you find a new word. See if you can figure out what a word means from its context. The *context* is the words, phrases, and sentences around the word you don't know.

Read this passage. What does *infinitesimal* mean?

from *Mrs. Piggle-Wiggle* by Betty MacDonald

At dinner that night, Allen cut his meat into such small pieces that his father looked over at him and said, "Perhaps you would like to borrow my magnifying glass? I am sure you are going to need it to see those infinitesimal bits of meat."

Could you tell that *infinitesimal* means "very, very small"? If you did, you probably used one of six kinds of context clues.

Kinds of Context Clues

1. **Synonyms**—words that mean the same as the new word
2. **Antonyms**—words that mean the opposite of the word
3. **Surrounding Sentences**—clues in other sentences
4. **Definitions**—statements of what a new word means
5. **Examples**—specific examples of a new word
6. **Repeated Words**—difficult words used more than once

Synonyms and Antonyms

Synonyms are different words with the same meaning. *Antonyms* are words that have the opposite meaning. Synonyms and antonyms give you good context clues about an unknown word. Look for them as you read.

Synonyms

Read the paragraph below. Can you figure out what the word *dormant* means?

> ### from *Volcano* by Patricia Lauber
>
> The earth has many volcanoes. Some are dead, or extinct, and will never erupt again. Some are active, giving off lava and gases. Many are sleeping, or dormant. They are quiet now, but at some time they will erupt again.

Maybe you figured it out without really knowing how you did it. A synonym for the unknown word *dormant* is given right before it. That synonym is *sleeping*. So *dormant* means "asleep."

Antonyms

Now figure out the meaning of a word by looking for an antonym. That's a word that means the opposite of the unknown word. Can you figure out what *slob* means in the passage below?

> ### from *Aldo Ice Cream* by Johanna Hurwitz
>
> "What will people think?" asked Elaine. "It makes us look like slobs."
>
> "No, it doesn't," said Karen reasonably. "It just looks as though Aldo is a slob." She looked at her brother, who was beginning his third ear of corn on the cob.
>
> "I'm not a slob," said Aldo, swallowing the corn in his mouth. "I'm very neat for a boy my age. And I had to work very hard to win."

Slob means "a messy person" or "someone who is not neat." You can tell because Aldo says he's not a slob. He's the opposite of that. He's very neat.

Surrounding Sentences

Sometimes you need to be patient to find context clues. The clues about a word's meaning won't always be in the same sentence. Often you will have to look around the whole paragraph to find clues. Read the paragraph below. What does the word *hoarders* mean?

from *Your Pet Hamster* by Elaine Landau

Words

Hamsters are hoarders. They like to store food. They fill their cheek pouches with food and then hide it in their cages for later. While you want to keep your pet's cage clean, do not continually remove the hoarded food. That would upset the animal. But don't feed your pet large amounts of any food that spoils quickly.

Let's say that you're not sure what *hoarders* means in that first sentence. Keep reading. The next sentences give you clues. They say that hamsters don't eat all their food at once. Instead, they hide some and keep it for later. A hoarder stores something for later use. If that's what you figured out, you're right!

context clue

context clue

context clue

MEANING

context clue

context clue

context clue

Definitions

Imagine you're reading and come to a word you don't know. First, look to see if the author gives you a definition of it.

In the passage below, what two terms are defined?

> ### from *Rain Forest Secrets* by Arthur Dorros
>
> Some scientists think that destroying the rain forests will make the whole earth's climate warmer. The warming is called the *greenhouse effect.*
>
> Rain forest trees and plants hold moisture. They breathe back into the air, or *transpire,* up to three-fourths of all the rain they get. This causes more rain. Cutting down rain forests reduces the amount of rain the earth receives. The land can become dry and barren.

The author defines the terms *greenhouse effect* and *transpire*. Notice that the terms being defined are printed in italics. Here the definitions come before the new terms. Sometimes the terms being defined will be in boldface, and the definitions will be in parentheses right after them. Look at this example.

They **transpire** *(or give off moisture) into the air.*

Examples

Often an author gives you examples. Look for signal words, such as *for example, such as, including, like,* and *especially*. They signal that you should look for examples.

Read the paragraph below. What does the word *wetlands* mean?

---

from *Discovery Works*

Wetlands include swamps, marshes, and bogs. People drain the water from wetlands to use the land for farming, housing, and industry. Today, less than half the wetlands in the United States remain.

Wetlands is not defined in this paragraph. You can tell what the word means because three examples of wetlands are given. It means a land that contains a lot of water, like a swamp, marsh, or bog.

Repeated Words

You may see a new word in one sentence and then you'll see it again a couple of sentences later. You might not figure out what it means the first time you see it. But you might be able to tell the next time it's used.

In the reading below, can you figure out what *genius* means?

> **from *I Was a Third Grade Science Project* by Mary Jane Auch**
>
> Having a genius for a friend can be real trouble. I know, because my best friend is Brian Lewis. All the other kids in third grade call him Brain. I don't, because he doesn't like it. He calls me Josh, even though some kids call me Birdbrain. It's not that I'm stupid, but when you hang around with a genius, you don't look like the smartest person in the world.

Did you figure out that a *genius* is a very smart person? The first time *genius* appears, it's hard to tell exactly what it means. By the end of the paragraph, you've learned that Brian is called Brain, like the brain in your head. You also know that Josh feels kind of dumb when he's around Brian. So, you should have a pretty good idea that Brian, a genius, is a very smart person.

Answering Vocabulary Questions

You've probably taken some vocabulary tests in school. If you haven't, you will soon. Learn how to read the questions on the test. Also, remember to rule out the answers that you know can't be right.

Definition Questions

Some questions ask you to pick the *best* definition for a word. Look at the example below.

Sample Question

1. <u>Unknowable</u> means:

    a. easy to understand
    b. not able to be understood
    c. confusion
    d. question

If you know some prefixes and suffixes, you can figure out what the answer is. The last part of the word, *able*, is a suffix. That suffix often makes a word into an adjective. So cross out answers **c** and **d,** because *confusion* and *question* are nouns. Do you see the word *know* inside the word *unknowable*? If you know that *un* means "not" and that *able* means "can do," you'll *know* that **b** is correct!

Words

Synonym and Antonym Questions

Sometimes tests ask you for synonyms or antonyms of words. Look at the examples below.

Synonym Questions

Remember that a synonym is a word with the same meaning as another. (*Synonym* starts with *s*, like *same*. You can remember it that way.) Try the example below.

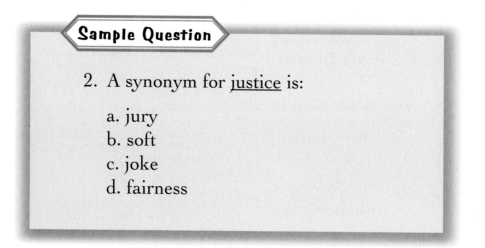

Sample Question

2. A synonym for <u>justice</u> is:

   a. jury
   b. soft
   c. joke
   d. fairness

What can you do if you have no idea what *justice* means? Look for any smaller parts or words in *justice*. How about *just*? Did you know that a *just* law means a fair law? Then you'd know answer **d** is correct.

Antonym Questions

A question that asks you for an antonym is asking for the *opposite* of a word. (*Antonym* starts with a vowel, and so does *opposite*. Try remembering it that way.) Look at this example.

> ## Sample Question
>
> 3. An antonym for <u>magnify</u> is:
>
>   a. reduce
>   b. clean
>   c. enlarge
>   d. hungry

Attack the problem in 3 steps.

1. Read the question and all of the answers.

2. Look at the word. Study its parts.

   Can you think of other words with *magn* in it? How about *magnificent*? That means "great." So maybe *magnify* has something to do with *great*.

3. Read each possible answer again. Do any of the words connect with *great*?

   You might start to pick answer **c** because *enlarge* sounds like it connects to being big or great. But be careful. Remember you want the opposite of *magnify*. Answer **a** is the best choice. *Reduce* is the opposite of *magnify*.

Paragraph Questions

Many vocabulary tests will give you a paragraph and ask you what a word means. Use context clues to answer this type of question. Try an example.

> ## from *McBroom Tells the Truth* by Sid Fleischman
>
> Just then a thin, long-legged man came ambling down the road. He was so scrawny I do believe he could have hidden behind a flagpole, ears and all. He wore a tall stiff collar, a diamond stickpin in his tie, and a straw hat.
>
> 4. <u>Scrawny</u> means:
>
>   a. poor
>   b. angry
>   c. skinny
>   d. delightful

You may not know the word *scrawny,* but try to figure it out from the context. From the first sentence, you know the man is thin and has long legs. Next, reread the sentence with *scrawny*. This time say "blank" instead of *scrawny*. What makes sense in the blank?

Then read another sentence. The words "hidden behind a flagpole" help you picture that he was thin. With this information, answer **c** makes the most sense.

Summing Up

- **The best way to build your vocabulary is to read as much as you can.**

- **When you come to a word you don't know, try several things to figure it out.**

  - **Break it into syllables.**

  - **Say each syllable and put the parts together.**

  - **Use what you know about prefixes, suffixes, and roots.**

- **Write down the new words you want to learn in a special Word Notebook.**

- **Use a dictionary. Look up words you don't know.**

- **Learn how to use context clues to help you figure out unknown words.**

Words

Understanding Paragraphs

- What Is a Paragraph?
- Paragraph Signals
- Finding the Subject
- Finding the Main Idea
- Kinds of Paragraphs
- How Paragraphs Are Organized

Paragraphs

111

Understanding Paragraphs

All stories and books are made up of paragraphs. If you understand paragraphs, you can be a better reader.

What Is a Paragraph?

A *paragraph* is a group of several sentences about the same subject. In stories, paragraphs tell you about a character or describe where the action takes place. In information books, paragraphs may tell you facts about the subject.

Paragraphs can be organized in different ways. Many paragraphs begin with a *topic sentence.* It tells what the paragraph is about and says the main point. The other sentences in a paragraph give details about that topic. The details in a paragraph support the topic sentence just as the legs of a table support the top.

Paragraph Signals

Writers signal where a new paragraph begins. Authors want to make this clear so you'll know the topic is changing. You may see one or both of these common paragraph signals.

Indenting
The first line of the new paragraph starts a few spaces to the right. This is called *indenting*.

Extra space
There's often an extra line of space right above a new paragraph.

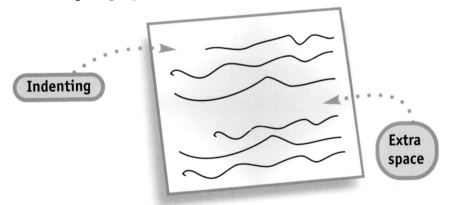

Indenting

Extra space

How to Understand Paragraphs

Remember that all the sentences in a paragraph are about one big idea. To understand what the paragraph is saying, you have to do two things.

1. Find the subject.
What is the paragraph about?

2. Figure out the main idea.
What does the author say about the subject?

Paragraphs

113

Finding the Subject

To find the subject of a paragraph, ask yourself what the paragraph is about. Look at three things.

1. The title or heading above the paragraph, if there is one

2. The first sentence

3. Names, repeated words, or important words

Take a look at the paragraph on the next page. See if you can tell what it's about.

Title

First sentence

repeated word

repeated word

Repeated or important words

SUBJECT

from *Trombones* by Bob Temple

Types of Trombone Music ◄ ········ Heading

Early trombones made lower, softer sounds than those used today. People played them in churches and the courts of kings and queens. Over time, the trombone's tubing was made wider, and the sound became livelier. Trombones began to be used by military bands and by orchestras in opera houses. Today, they are used in all types of bands, including marching bands and jazz bands. Would you like to play the trombone?

First sentence

Repeated words

Paragraphs

You can see that the word *trombone* is repeated several times. Also, all the sentences give details about trombones. It isn't hard to tell the subject of this paragraph is trombones, is it?

Now you know how to find the subject of a paragraph. Next, you'll learn how to figure out the main idea of a paragraph.

Finding the Main Idea

The *main idea* is what the author says about the subject of the paragraph. It is the point the author wants you to understand.

Sometimes the author tells the main idea right in the first sentence. In paragraphs like that, it's easy to find what the main idea is! In other types of paragraphs, the main idea is not so easy to find. You have to figure it out.

Main Idea in First Sentence

Look at the paragraph on the next page. Read the first sentence. It tells you both the subject and the main idea. Just ask yourself, "What is this about?"

First
sentence

from *Koalas* by Emilie U. Lepthien

Main idea

Koalas can be noisy. They grunt and growl and make clicking noises. When they are hurt, they sound almost like human babies crying.

You can tell right away that this paragraph is about koalas. Now ask yourself, "What is the author saying about koalas?" Finding the main idea of this paragraph is not too hard. The author says it right in the first sentence.

In this paragraph, the author says koalas can be noisy. The other sentences give details about three kinds of noises koalas make.

Paragraphs

from *Koalas*

Subject

Koalas can be noisy. They grunt and growl and make clicking noises. When they are hurt, they sound almost like human babies crying.

Three details

Main Idea in Last Sentence

What do you do when the main idea of the paragraph is not in the first sentence? Then look for the main idea in the last sentence. Some authors like to give you the details first. Later, they show you what all those details mean.

As you read, keep in mind what the subject is. When you get to the last sentence, you'll see what the author is saying about the subject.

Now read the paragraph on the next page. Then see if you can tell what the main idea is.

Last sentence

from "Out of Sight, Out of Mind"

Details

A frog lays thousands of jelly-covered eggs. Many frog eggs become food for other animals. The frog eggs that do survive develop into tadpoles. Some tadpoles become food for snakes. Although a frog lays thousands of eggs, few eggs survive to develop into adult frogs. Laying many eggs, then, is an adaptation that helps frogs survive as a species.

Main idea

Paragraphs

What's the subject? You probably had no trouble telling that the subject is frog eggs. *Frog* and *eggs* appear in almost every sentence.

How did you figure out what the author is saying about frog eggs? It probably seemed like the author was saying a bunch of different things. But, in the last sentence, the author sums up all the details into the main idea. Laying many eggs helps the frog species survive. That's because a lot of eggs and tadpoles get eaten by other animals.

Implied Main Idea

Sometimes the author doesn't say the main idea in the first sentence or in the last sentence. When the main idea is not stated directly, it is *implied*. That means the reader has to figure it out. You have to act like a detective and put all of the clues together. As a reader, you think about how the details in each of the sentences fit together.

The paragraph below is from a book about the life of Booker T. Washington. He was a famous African-American teacher and leader. As you read it, try to figure out what the author is saying about Booker T. Washington.

> ### from *Booker T. Washington* by Patricia and Fredrick McKissack
>
> The school was 500 miles away. Booker walked in the rain. He slept on the ground. He hopped trains, and begged for rides on the back of wagons. It was a long, hard trip. But he would not turn back.
>
> **Details**

This paragraph gives details about Booker's trip to a faraway school. But the main idea of the paragraph is about more than just that. What does the author have to say *about* Booker? Use a Web to help you make sense of details.

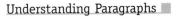

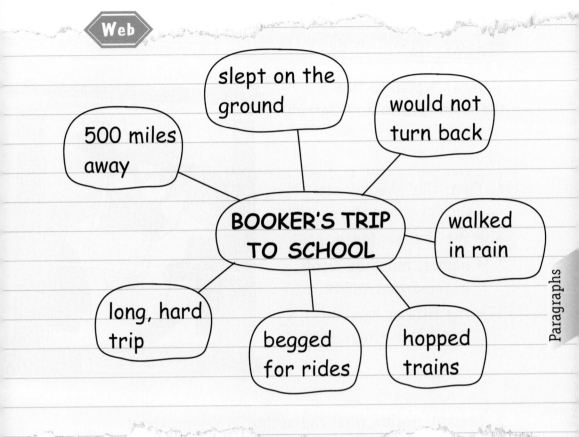

Paragraphs

Look at the details. To get to school, Booker T. Washington had to walk in the rain, sleep on the ground, hop on trains, and beg for rides on wagons. The author says it was a "long, hard trip." The author also says, in the last sentence, that Booker "would not turn back."

If you add up all these details, you can conclude that Booker was *determined* to get to school. He wouldn't let anything stop him. That's the main idea of the paragraph. Even though the author did not say this directly, you can figure it out.

Here's a plan to find
the main idea in a paragraph.

1. First, find the subject.
Look for these clues.
   - the first sentence
   - names, repeated words,
     or important words
   - the title or heading
     above the paragraph

2. Second, decide what the author is saying about
the subject. Ask yourself these questions.
   - "What does the author say about the subject
     in the first sentence?"
   - "What does the author
     say about the subject in
     the last sentence?"
   - "What do the details
     tell me about
     the subject?"

3. Third, put together the subject and what the author is saying about it. In your own words, tell the main idea.

4. Use a simple organizer to keep track of what the paragraph is about.

- Write the subject at the top.
- Next, write the main idea.
- List the details in smaller boxes.

Main Idea Organizer

SUBJECT		
MAIN IDEA		
DETAIL	DETAIL	DETAIL

Kinds of Paragraphs

You have probably noticed that paragraphs can be very different from one another. Some are long, and some are short. Some describe a place or a character. Others list facts or give an opinion. Understanding the different kinds of paragraphs can help you figure out the main idea more quickly and easily.

How to Understand Paragraphs

1. Narrative paragraphs tell a story.

2. Descriptive paragraphs describe a person, place, or thing.

3. Persuasive paragraphs give an opinion about something.

4. Expository paragraphs give information and explain ideas.

Narrative Paragraphs

Narrative paragraphs tell stories about what happens to people. Read the narrative paragraph below. As you do, watch for details about what happened to this family one summer afternoon.

from *The Gold Cadillac* by Mildred D. Taylor

We waited. More than three hours we waited. Finally my father came out of the police station. We had lots of questions to ask him. He said the police had given him a ticket for speeding and locked him up. But then the judge had come. My father had paid the ticket and they had let him go.

Details

Paragraphs

This narrative paragraph tells about a series of events. It's the story of what happened to a family one day after the police stopped their car. You can summarize this paragraph by listing the different details.

Summary Notes

- The family waited a long time for the father.
- The police had given him a ticket for speeding.
- They put him in jail.
- After the judge came, the father paid the ticket and left.

Descriptive Paragraphs

A good descriptive paragraph uses words to paint a picture in your mind. For instance, the paragraph below describes an unusual object. As you read, watch for details that help you see what it looks like.

**from *Knights of the Kitchen Table*
by Jon Scieszka**

Details

And it was a book. But it wasn't like any book I had ever seen before. It was such a dark, dark blue that it looked almost black, like the sky at night. It had gold stars and moons along the back edge, and twisting silver designs on the front and back that looked like writing from a long time ago.

This paragraph is full of details about what a mysterious book looks like. You can use a Web to list the important parts of the description.

Web

dark, dark blue — BOOK — like the night sky

gold stars and moons

silver designs like old writing

Persuasive Paragraphs

A persuasive paragraph gives the author's opinion. The author tries to get you to agree with him or her. Can you tell what the writer here wants you to believe?

from *What We Can Do About Litter* by Donna Bailey

1 Many of the goods we buy are wrapped several times. Bags of chips come packed within larger cellophane wrappers and fruit is often put on trays covered in plastic. To **2** help reduce garbage and litter, do not buy things that have more wrapping than is really needed.

Details

Author's opinion

Paragraphs

The author's opinion comes in the last sentence. The author tries to persuade you to stop buying things that have extra wrapping. As you read, make a list of what you learn. It will help you keep track of what a persuasive paragraph is about.

Summary Notes

AUTHOR'S OPINION

We should not buy things with too much wrapping.

1. Many things come with extra wrapping.
2. Extra wrapping means more garbage.

Expository Paragraphs

Expository paragraphs explain things. The writer of an expository paragraph gives readers information about a subject. For example, this paragraph explains all about tree bark.

from *A Tree Is Growing* by Arthur Dorros

Facts

Bark is the skin of a tree. The outer layer of bark protects the tree. When an oak tree is young, the bark is as smooth as a baby's skin. As the tree grows older, the bark becomes rough and cracked.

This paragraph explains what tree bark is, how it helps a tree, and how it looks and feels over time. Here is one way to keep track of some of the facts.

Web

How Paragraphs Are Organized

For a writer, organizing a paragraph is a big job. It involves deciding what details or facts to put in the paragraph and what order to put them in. But, if you understand the ways of organizing paragraphs, you can read them faster and understand more. You will know what to expect. You'll also know where the most important information is while you're reading.

Here are five common ways to organize paragraphs.

Paragraphs

Ways of Organizing Paragraphs

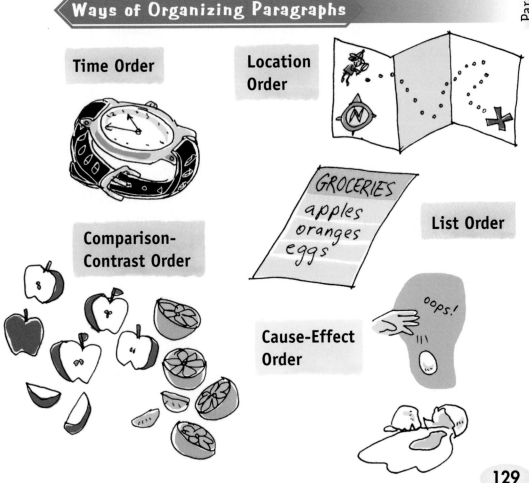

Time Order

Location Order

GROCERIES
apples
oranges
eggs

List Order

Comparison-Contrast Order

Cause-Effect Order

oops!

129

Time Order

Time order means the author is telling events in the order in which they happened. It's easy to follow paragraphs that use time order. Nothing skips around or seems out of place. For example, read this paragraph about the invention of the telephone.

from *Cyber Space* by David Jefferis

Three different times

In 1876, inventor Alexander Graham Bell developed the telephone, which let people speak over the wires. This new invention was a great success. In 1880, there were just 33,000 telephones in the world. Ten years later, there were nearly half a million.

The paragraph about the telephone tells about what happened in a period of 15 years. Look for words that show time, like the dates 1876 and 1880. Look also for other words that show time, such as "ten years later." Many clues signal time order. Here are some examples.

Time Clues

- times of the day
- days of the week
- months
- years

- *before*
- *after*
- *then*
- *later*

- *next*
- *first*
- *last*

Timeline

1876   1880   1890

| the telephone invented | only 33,000 phones in the world | almost half a million phones in the world |

In your notebook, you can create a Timeline like the one above. It shows the order of the events in the paragraph. Notice that the paragraph tells about three different times and what happened in each one.

Paragraphs

Location Order

When authors describe a place, they want you to be able to see what it looks like. To help you see it, authors carefully arrange the details. They use an order that makes sense. They go from top to bottom, from left to right, or in a circle. Here's an example of how one author describes the view from a tree house.

from *Dinosaurs Before Dark* by Mary Pope Osborne

"Look. You can see far, far away," said Annie. She was peering out the tree house window.

View on one side

Jack looked out the window with her. Down below were the tops of the other trees. In the distance he saw the Frog Creek library. The elementary school. The park.

Annie pointed in the other direction. "There's our house," she said.

View on the other side

You can easily draw a picture or make a map of this scene. Just use the details in these paragraphs. In your notebook, sketch out what you think the scene looks like.

Picture of the Scene

The description of the scene has two main parts. First, you learn about the view in one direction—the trees, the library, the school, and the park. Then, in the last sentence, you find out their house is in the other direction.

Paragraphs

133

List Order

Sometimes authors put their facts and examples in a list. Paragraphs organized in list order give lots of details but in no particular order. In this paragraph, the author lists interesting facts about crows.

from _Crows! Strange and Wonderful_ by Laurence Pringle

Facts

❶ Crows tease other animals. Sometimes a crow gives a playful nip to the tail of a dog or other animal, then flies out of reach. ❷ Crows also mimic the calls of other birds. They imitate all sorts of other sounds—a squeaky door, a puppy's yelp, a cat's meow. ❸ Tame crows can be taught to say such words as "hello," "good-bye," and "hot dog."

You can make a simple list like this to help you remember these facts about crows.

List

CROWS
- tease other animals
- make sounds
- can be taught to say words

Or, you may want to list facts in a Web.

Web

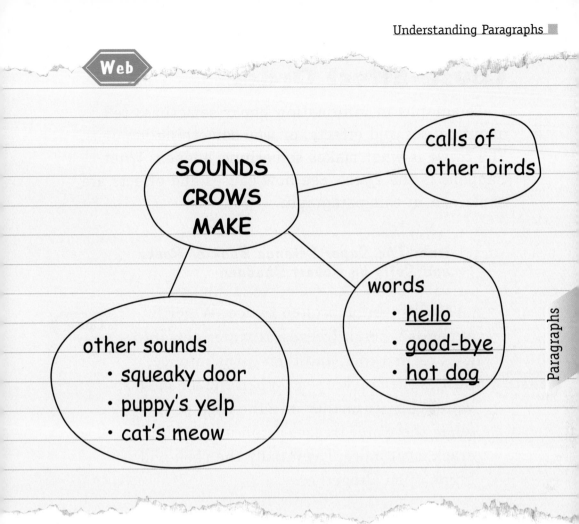

SOUNDS CROWS MAKE

calls of other birds

words
- <u>hello</u>
- <u>good-bye</u>
- <u>hot dog</u>

other sounds
- squeaky door
- puppy's yelp
- cat's meow

Paragraphs

You can make your Web as simple or as detailed as you want. This Web shows the kinds of sounds that crows make.

Cause-Effect Order

Paragraphs in information books sometimes tell about causes and effects, or *why* something happens. The *cause* is what makes something happen. What happens is the *effect*. See how causes and effects are explained in this paragraph.

> **from *The Super Science Book of Rocks and Soils* by Robert Snedden**
>
> Rocks can be broken by ice. Water expands when it freezes. **Cause** If water gets into a crack in a rock and then turns into ice, it **Effect** pushes the crack open. When the ice melts, water can get farther into the rock so that when the water freezes again it opens the crack a bit more. Eventually the rock will break open altogether.

Use a Cause-Effect Organizer to help you understand what happens when water gets into a rock. In your notes, create a simple organizer.

Cause-Effect Organizer

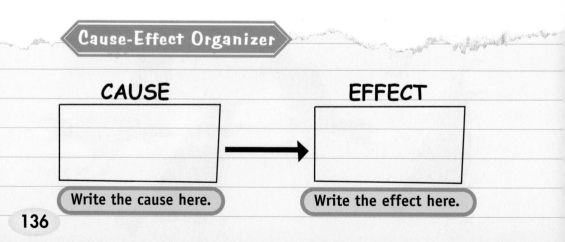

CAUSE → EFFECT

Write the cause here. Write the effect here.

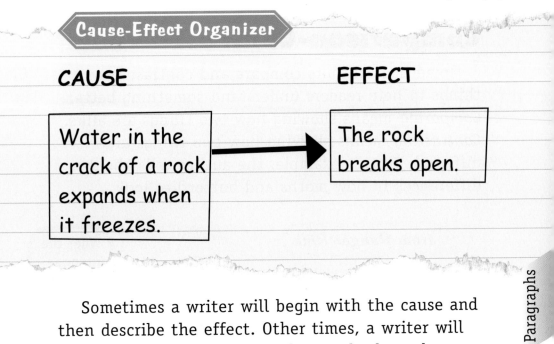

Sometimes a writer will begin with the cause and then describe the effect. Other times, a writer will explain the effect first and then go back to the cause. Remember, a paragraph may be about more than one cause and more than one effect.

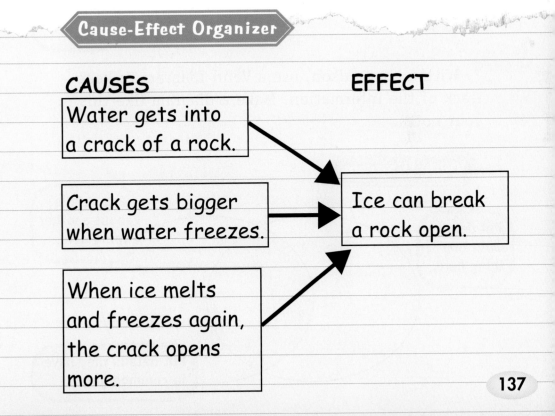

Paragraphs

Comparison-Contrast Order

Sometimes authors compare and contrast two things to help readers understand something better. *Comparing* means showing how two things are alike. *Contrasting* means showing how two things are different. In this example, the author tells about differences in how moths and butterflies look.

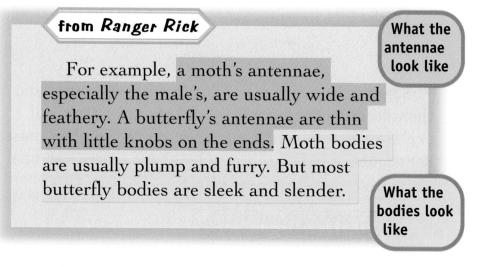

from *Ranger Rick*

What the antennae look like

For example, a moth's antennae, especially the male's, are usually wide and feathery. A butterfly's antennae are thin with little knobs on the ends. Moth bodies are usually plump and furry. But most butterfly bodies are sleek and slender.

What the bodies look like

With a comparison, use a Venn Diagram to keep track of the information. Make a diagram like this in your notes.

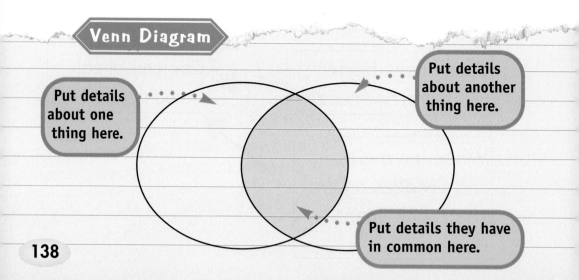

Venn Diagram

Put details about one thing here.

Put details about another thing here.

Put details they have in common here.

Venn Diagram

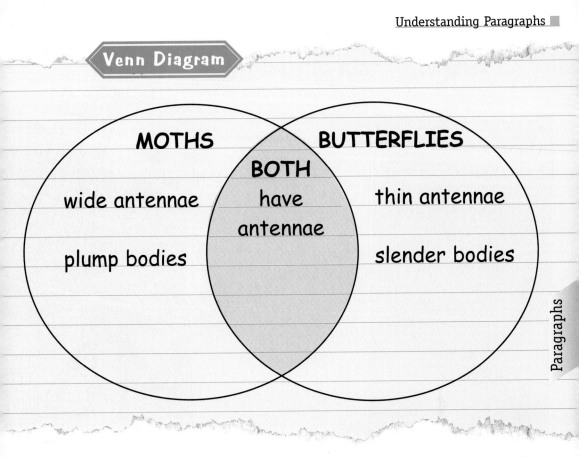

Paragraphs

Did you notice that only one detail is in the shaded part of the circles? That's because the paragraph doesn't really say much about how moths and butterflies look alike.

Summing Up

- **Paragraphs are groups of sentences about the same subject.**

- **As you read, find the subject and figure out the main idea of each paragraph.**

- **Look for clues about how paragraphs are organized. The more you know about kinds of paragraphs, the easier it will be to read and understand them.**

Reading for
Information

Reading Nonfiction
Reading an Article
Reading a Biography

Focus on Nonfiction
Focus on Information Books
Focus on a Website
Focus on Graphics

Elements of Nonfiction

Information

Reading an Article

Do you know how monkeys live in the jungle? Have you ever wondered what causes a tornado? Where do you go to find information about those subjects? Is it the library? Is it a computer? Is it an encyclopedia? These are all good places to find information.

The reading process can help you find information more easily. Use it when you read an article at home, at school, in the library, and on the computer.

Goals

Here you'll learn how to:

✔ **read and understand the information in** articles

✔ **use the strategy of** summarizing

Before Reading

You might read an article for all kinds of reasons. Sometimes you're reading just for fun, and you can zip your way through.

Other times, you're reading for school. Then you need to slow down and pay close attention to what you're doing.

A Set a Purpose

The title of an article can help you decide on a reading purpose. Turn the title of the article into a question. For example, what could be your reading purpose for an article titled "Bubble, Bubble, Spittlebug"?

■ **What is a spittlebug?**
■ **Where do spittlebugs live?**
■ **What do bubbles have to do with spittlebugs?**

B Preview

Now preview "Bubble, Bubble, Spittlebug." As you preview, look for the items on this checklist:

Preview Checklist

✔ title and any headings
✔ first and last paragraphs
✔ illustrations and photos
✔ words in boldface

Information

Bubble, Bubble, Spittlebug

By Beverly J. Letchworth

PREVIEW
Title

In spring, you may have seen white foam on an evergreen tree or other plant. It looks like spit!

PREVIEW
First paragraph

The foam is where young spittlebugs live. These insects are protected by the foam. They usually don't do much harm to the plants.

Who is hiding in that foam?

Baby bugs are living in that foam.

PREVIEW
Boldface words

PREVIEW
Photo

144

"Bubble, Bubble, Spittlebug," continued

Spittlebugs eat plant juices.

PREVIEW

Photo

Once the bugs have grown into adults, they stop making foam. They leave their homes and jump from plant to plant in search of food. The adults look a little like tiny frogs. For this reason they are also called froghoppers.

If you see some foam on a plant, you might want to take a careful look inside. Gently push some of the foam aside with a twig. Deep inside you may see a few insects eating plant juice. They might also be making more bubbles. Be sure to push the foam back after a moment to cover the insects and keep them safe.

A mother spittlebug lays her eggs on the plant in late summer. The babies hatch in spring. They begin to eat juices from the plant.

The babies eat more juice than their bodies need for food. The extra juice mixes with a special substance that the spittlebugs produce. When this fluid is released, it mixes with the air, forming a bubbly foam.

What is so great about having a foam home? The space inside is moist to keep the bugs' soft bodies from drying out. And the foam tastes bad, so it keeps away most animals that would eat the bugs.

Some birds will stick their beaks through the foam to find the bugs. Wasps and ants might eat them, too. But most of the bugs stay safe inside the foam.

Soon the spittlebugs will grow up and leave their foam home. They will join the other insects in the meadow.

PREVIEW

Last paragraph

Adult spittlebugs are shaped a little like frogs.

PREVIEW

Photo

Information

C Plan

What did you learn from your preview?

- Baby spittlebugs live in foam bubbles.
- When they grow up, spittlebugs leave the foam.

Your list might be different from this one. But don't worry. You didn't miss anything. During your careful reading, you will learn lots more important details.

After previewing, choose a reading strategy that will help you make sense of the article. Articles usually have lots of information you'll want to remember.

Reading Strategy: Summarizing

Summarizing means telling the main points in your own words. It's a good strategy to use with an article. Summarizing helps you separate important from unimportant details. Use a 5 W's and H Organizer to sort out what you learn.

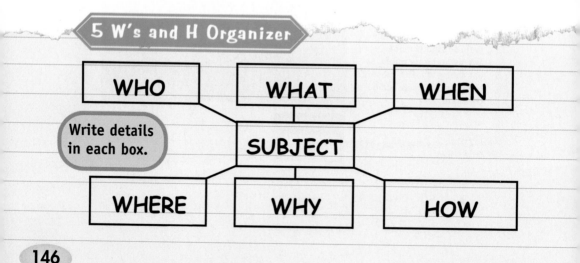

5 W's and H Organizer

WHO	WHAT	WHEN

Write details in each box.

SUBJECT

WHERE	WHY	HOW

During Reading

Now you are ready to do a slow and careful reading of "Bubble, Bubble, Spittlebug."

D Read with a Purpose

Keep your 5 W's and H Organizer on the desk in front of you as you read. Write notes in the boxes as you go.

Find the Subject

The first step when you read an article is to find the subject. It is what the writer is mostly talking about.

What is the subject of this article? If you decided the subject has to do with spittlebugs, you're right! How do you find the subject of an article? These tips can help.

Information

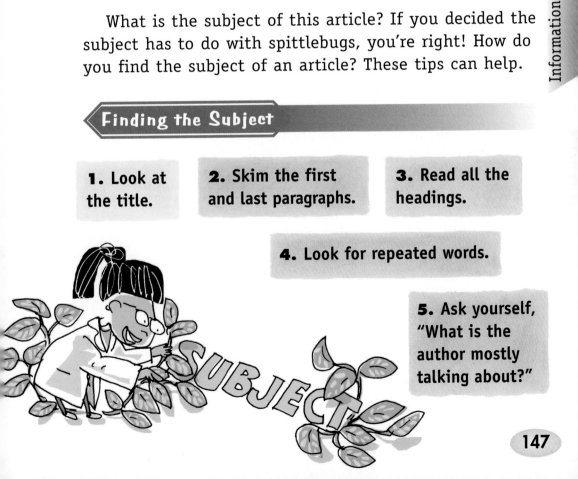

Finding the Subject

1. Look at the title.

2. Skim the first and last paragraphs.

3. Read all the headings.

4. Look for repeated words.

5. Ask yourself, "What is the author mostly talking about?"

Find What the Author Says about the Subject

After you find the subject of the article, you need to figure out what the author is saying about it. What details does the author give? Which of these details are most important? Use your 5 W's and H Organizer. It will help you find *who, what, when, where, why,* and *how.*

from "Bubble, Bubble, Spittlebug"

Where

Who

When

A mother spittlebug lays her eggs on the plant in late summer. The babies hatch in spring. They begin to eat juices from the plant.

How

The babies eat more juice than their bodies need for food. The extra juice mixes with a special substance that the spittlebugs produce. When this fluid is released, it mixes with the air, forming a bubbly foam.

What

Why

What is so great about having a foam home? The space inside is moist to keep the bugs' soft bodies from drying out. And the foam tastes bad, so it keeps away most animals that would eat the bugs.

Finding answers to the 5 W's and H questions makes it easier to spot the most important details. Your finished organizer might look something like the one on the next page.

5 W's and H Organizer

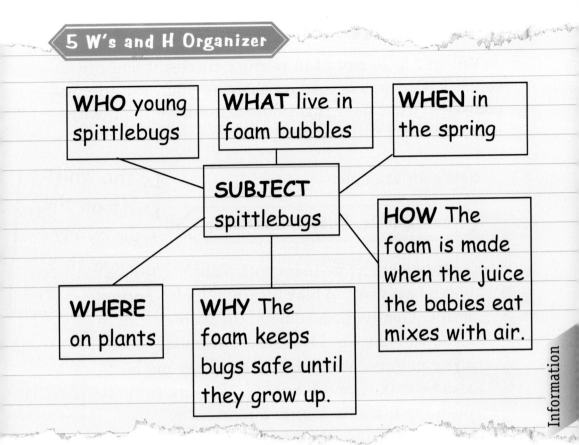

Information

Draw a Conclusion

Now you've learned some facts about spittlebugs. Have you understood the main idea? What conclusion can you draw? Ask yourself, "What is the main idea or message in the article?"

| subject | + | what the author says about the subject | = | main idea |

| young spittlebugs | + | live in foam bubbles they make | = | Young spittlebugs make foam homes that keep them safe. |

E Connect

You will have more fun reading articles if you can connect what you're reading about to your own life. Ask yourself, "What does this information have to do with me? What do I think about this?"

Here's an example.

from "Bubble, Bubble, Spittlebug"

If you see some foam on a plant, you might want to take a careful look inside. Gently push some of the foam aside with a twig. Deep inside you may see a few insects eating plant juice. They might also be making more bubbles. Be sure to push the foam back after a moment to cover the insects and keep them safe.

Is the white stuff on the tree by my garage this foam?

I bet some bugs try to leave before you cover them up.

After Reading

Now decide whether you've learned all that you need to learn from the article.

F Pause and Reflect

Take a minute to think about what you just read. Can you answer questions like these?

- **Can I list three to four facts I learned?**
- **Can I tell the main idea in my own words?**
- **Are there parts I don't understand?**

Write out any questions you still have. Then reread parts of the article to answer your questions.

> Information

My Questions

- Are the bugs totally safe in the foam?
- How long do the bugs live in the foam?
- What happens to the foam when the bugs leave?

151

G Reread

Reread the parts that you had questions about or that were most confusing. For example, maybe you weren't sure how safe the bugs are. Read over that part slowly and carefully. Take notes.

from "Bubble, Bubble, Spittlebug"

Some birds will stick their beaks through the foam to find the bugs. Wasps and ants might eat them, too. But most of the bugs stay safe inside the foam.

Some bugs get eaten.

Use a Main Idea Organizer to list the most important information. First, write what you think the main idea is. Then, write the details. If you can't come up with three details, you may need to think again about the main idea.

Main Idea Organizer

MAIN IDEA Young spittlebugs make foam homes that keep them safe.		
DETAIL The foam is made from extra plant juices.	DETAIL The foam protects their bodies.	DETAIL Most animals keep away from the foam.

H Remember

No one can remember everything in an article. That's why you need to make some notes after your reading. After all, what's the point of reading if you forget everything later? Try telling a friend what you learned.

Another good way to remember what you've read is to make Summary Notes. Summary Notes can help you keep track of the most important points.

Summary Notes

"Bubble, Bubble, Spittlebug"

1. Baby spittlebugs live in white foam on plants.
2. The foam is made from juices.
3. Most animals stay away from it.
4. Adult spittlebugs stop making the foam. They get big and move away.

Information

Summing Up

When you read an article, remember to use the reading process and the strategy of **summarizing**. Use one of these tools to help you keep track of what you learn:

- 5 W's and H Organizer
- Summary Notes
- Main Idea Organizer

Reading a Biography

How can you find out about someone famous? How can you learn about someone you never met? The answer is that you can read a biography. A *biography* is the true story of someone's life.

Biographies are packed full of details. They tell about where people lived, who their families were, and what they liked to do. In a biography, you learn what a person is like and why he or she is famous.

Before Reading

A good biography can make you feel like you really know the person you're reading about. One way to know a person is to find out about events in his or her life.

A Set a Purpose

Sometimes you'll read a biography because you're curious about someone's life. Other times you'll read for a school assignment. In both cases, your purpose is the same. You want to learn about the person's life and find out what he or she was really like.

■ **What kind of life did this person have?**

■ **What was he or she really like?**

B Preview

Here you'll read part of a biography of Benjamin Franklin. Have you heard of him? Even if you already know a little about him, take the time to preview. Look for the items on this checklist:

Preview Checklist

✔ front and back covers of the book
✔ table of contents and chapter titles
✔ opening paragraphs
✔ photographs and pictures
✔ key dates, names, and places

Information

Front Cover

BENJAMIN FRANKLIN

Printer, Inventor, Statesman
A FIRST BIOGRAPHY

by DAVID A. ADLER

illustrated by Lyle Miller

PREVIEW
Title and author

PREVIEW
Picture

PREVIEW
Chapter titles

Story moves from when he was young to when he dies.

CONTENTS

Key Dates

IMPORTANT DATES

PREVIEW

Born in 1706

1706	Born on January 17 in Boston.
1718–1723	Worked in his brother's print shop.
1722	"Silence Dogood" letters published in the *New England Courant*.
1728	Opened his own print shop in Philadelphia.
1729	Bought and began to publish the *Pennsylvania Gazette*.
1730	Married Deborah Read on September 1.
1730 or 1731	Son William born. (The exact date is unknown.)
1731	Set up a circulating library in Philadelphia, perhaps the first in America.
1732–1758	Published *Poor Richard's Almanack*.
1732	
1736–1751	
1743	
1752	

Opening Paragraphs

1. *One Sunday Morning on Milk Street*

PREVIEW

Places

PREVIEW

Dates

In 1706, the year Benjamin Franklin was born, Boston was the largest city in the thirteen American colonies. More than ten thousand people lived there in some three thousand houses. There were one hundred streets, lanes, and alleys. Among them were King and Queen streets (the colonies were still loyal to the king and queen of England), School Street, Winter and Summer Streets, Milk Street, and Water Street.

On Sunday morning, January 17, 1706, Boston's one hundred streets, lanes, and alleys were covered with snow. Just three days before, a fierce storm had hit the city. The snow was so deep that one man was actually lost in it and died. On that Sunday, in a four-room house on Milk Street, Josiah Franklin saw his fifteenth child and tenth son born. Later that day, Josiah carried the baby across the street to the Old South Church, where he was baptized.

PREVIEW

Names

Information

C Plan

What did you learn during your preview?

■ Franklin was born in 1706.

■ He was from Boston.

■ Where he lived had lots of streets.

As soon as you finish your preview, decide what reading strategy to use. Remember your purpose. It is to find out as much as you can about Benjamin Franklin and his life. What strategy should you use?

Reading Strategy: Note-taking

With any biography, you have a lot to keep track of when you read. The strategy of note-taking can help. That means you will write down facts and details that seem important. Key Word Notes can help you remember what you're reading about. Before reading, divide a sheet of paper into two parts.

Key Word Notes

KEY WORDS	NOTES

List words here.   Write about them here.

During Reading

As you read, remember your purpose. You want to get an idea of what Benjamin Franklin was really like and what kind of life he had.

D Read with a Purpose

On the next couple of pages you will read part of a biography of Ben Franklin. Watch for important details about his life.

Find the Key Topics

Every biography is different. But most of them cover at least some of the same key topics:

- family and friends
- school
- jobs
- major setbacks or problems
- personality
- achievements

Now read about Franklin. What key topics can you find?

from *Benjamin Franklin* by David A. Adler

At age ten, Benjamin's father removed him from school altogether and made him work in his soap and candle shop. There Benjamin cut wicks for the candles, filled the dipping molds, helped look after the shop, and went on errands.

Family and school

Job

Information

159

from *Benjamin Franklin*

Job   In 1728, at age twenty-two, Benjamin Franklin had his own print shop and he meant to make it a success. He not only was serious and worked hard, but he made sure the people of Philadelphia knew it. He dressed plainly and was careful not to **Personality** be seen standing about and talking. He never went fishing or shooting and only occasionally read a book in public. Sometimes, to show that he was not above doing any of the work necessary for his shop, he pushed a wheelbarrow piled high with paper through the streets of Philadelphia. He also paid his bills promptly, so people were happy to do business with him.

To make Key Word Notes, list key words or topics on the left. Try to leave writing space between each one. Make your notes on the right. Here's an example.

Key Word Notes

KEY WORDS	NOTES
Family and school	• Father made him leave school at age ten.
Jobs	• First job was in his father's shop. • Later, he owned his own print shop.

Find Details about the Person

Most biographies have lots of names, dates, and events. But they're only part of the story. One reason you read a biography is to find out what someone is really like. As you read more about Benjamin Franklin, ask yourself questions about him.

- What does Ben Franklin say and do?
- How does he feel?
- What do others think about him?
- How do I feel about him?

Information

from *Benjamin Franklin*

He was postmaster of Philadelphia and later postmaster general of the colonies. Franklin also set up the first fire company in Philadelphia and the first police force in the colonies. In 1741 he advertised a new stove he had designed, the Franklin stove, which did a better job of heating a house than a fireplace and used less fuel. He didn't take out a patent on the stove. He didn't want to make a profit from helping people keep warm.

> He did many different things.

> He cared about people.

Look for Cause and Effect

The events in your life can shape the sort of person you become. Part of the fun in reading a biography comes in seeing what events shaped a person's life. Look for cause and effect as you read this description of Benjamin Franklin.

from *Benjamin Franklin*

What he did

When he was seven he bought a whistle, and learned the value of money. His brothers and sisters laughed at him and said he had paid too much for it. Benjamin cried. He was sorry he had spent the money. Years later he wrote, "A penny saved is two pence clear," "Get what you can and what you get hold," and "Save what you may, no morning sun lasts the whole day." During the rest of his life, Benjamin was careful not to spend more money than necessary on anything.

How it affected him

Use a Cause-Effect Organizer to show how one thing caused something else.

Cause-Effect Organizer

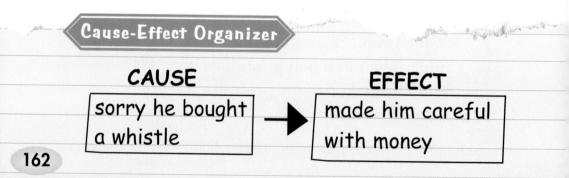

CAUSE

sorry he bought a whistle

→

EFFECT

made him careful with money

162

E Connect

When you read a biography, try to connect what you're reading about to your own life. Ask yourself questions like these.

Do I know anyone like this?

How do I feel about this person?

Has anything like this ever happened to me?

Keep track of your own opinions as you read. Write your thoughts on sticky notes. When you finish reading, look at your notes and decide how you feel about the person. Share your ideas with friends. Do they have the same opinions?

Information

from *Benjamin Franklin*

Even at the age of seventy-nine, Franklin was still curious, still fascinated, by the world around him. On the sea voyage home, he measured the temperature of the ocean water at different depths. He noted the currents. He made a long list of suggestions for safer sailing.

I really like him. He knew a lot of different things.

163

After Reading

As soon as you finish reading a biography, stop to think about what you learned.

F Pause and Reflect

Ask yourself questions about what you read.

- **What are some important events in this person's life?**
- **How do I feel about the person?**

G Reread

To answer these questions about a reading, you will probably have to reread. To find out more about Franklin's interest in science, find the part about his experiments. Start rereading there.

---

from Benjamin Franklin

In June 1752, he conducted his famous kite and lightning experiment. He made a kite out of silk and two sticks. From the top of the kite, he attached a wire to act as a lightning catcher. To the string he attached a silk ribbon and a key. His son William flew the kite in the midst of a storm. Lightning hit the wire. Benjamin Franklin touched the key and felt a spark. He had proved that lightning is electricity.

> Franklin's kite experiment

> What he found out

H Remember

The notes you take will help you remember what you read. Look them over. Then try writing down some of the things you learned.

Making a Timeline of key dates and events is an easy way to organize what you learned in a biography.

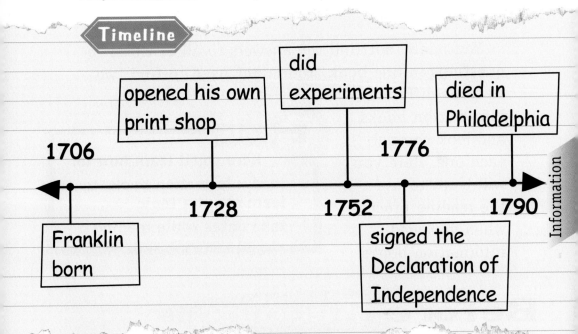

Timeline

did experiments

opened his own print shop

died in Philadelphia

1706   1776

1728   1752   1790

Franklin born

signed the Declaration of Independence

Information

S umming Up

Use the strategy of **note-taking** when you read a biography. Think about the events that shaped the person's life and what he or she was really like. Use these three useful tools for remembering information:

∎ Key Word Notes   ∎ Timeline
∎ Cause-Effect Organizer

Focus on Information Books

What is the longest river in the world? What animals live in rivers? Where does water in a river come from? All of these questions are about rivers, but each one asks for different information about rivers.

You might not find the answers to all of these questions in one book. You might need to find two or three different information books and look through each one. Here you will learn to use the reading process when you read information books.

Goals

Here you'll learn how to:
- ✔ **read information books to learn about a topic**
- ✔ **take notes while reading**

Before Reading

At some point, your teacher will give you an assignment where you will need to do research. You'll have to use information books to answer the questions.

Understand Your Purpose

Before you even pick up a book, read the assignment carefully. Learn what information you need to find out. What if you had to do a report on pandas? Look at this assignment.

Animal Report Assignment

1. Describe what pandas look like.
2. Explain what pandas eat.
3. Tell where pandas live.

For your reading purpose, turn your assignment into specific questions. Here are some questions about what pandas look like.

- What color are pandas?
- How big are pandas?
- What do their faces look like?

Choose Information Books

First, go to the library and choose books that tell about pandas. Preview each book. Make sure it will be helpful to you. Skim each book quickly.

LOOK IN THESE PARTS OF EACH BOOK

✔ table of contents
✔ pictures
✔ headings
✔ index

Information

During Reading

First, check that a book has information you need. Then start reading. Keep a pencil and paper or note cards handy so you can take notes.

Look for Key Details

When reading for information, you can read the whole book or just part of it. As you read, remember your purpose questions. Let's say you are trying to find out what a panda looks like. What do you learn from reading this page?

How big a panda is

Giant pandas weigh between 200 and 300 pounds (90 to 135 kilograms) and stand on all four legs. If one stood next to you, it would only come up to your waist.

Pandas walk on all four legs.

This one short paragraph is useful. It gives you some key details about what pandas look like.

Take Notes

Write down the facts you find. You just read a paragraph that tells how big pandas are and how they stand. Keep track of this information by writing Summary Notes.

Start by writing the subject. Then make a list of the details you want to remember.

Information

Summary Notes

PANDAS
What They Look Like
1. They weigh between 200 and 300 pounds.
2. When they stand on all four legs, they come up to my waist.

You now have *some* facts about what pandas look like. But that does not give you a complete picture. You will need to keep reading to find the rest of the information for your report.

Remember Your Purpose

Go back and look at the list of specific questions on page 167. Ask yourself if you have answered them. You know that pandas weigh a lot and stand on all fours. But what color are pandas? What do their faces look like?

You may need to use another book about pandas to find more information. Read this part of a different book for more details of what a panda looks like.

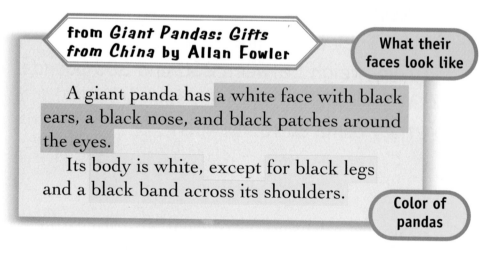

from *Giant Pandas: Gifts from China* by Allan Fowler

What their faces look like

A giant panda has a white face with black ears, a black nose, and black patches around the eyes.

Its body is white, except for black legs and a black band across its shoulders.

Color of pandas

This paragraph gives you new facts about what pandas look like. Add these details to your Summary Notes. You can even make a little sketch to help you remember what you learned.

Summary Notes

PANDAS
What They Look Like

1. They weigh between 200 and 300 pounds.
2. When they stand on all four legs, they come up to my waist.
3. They have a white face with a black nose.
4. They have black ears and black patches on the eyes.
5. The body is white.
6. The legs and shoulders are black.

Information

At this point, you may decide you have enough information. You can describe what pandas look like. But the assignment had two other parts. For the report, you also need facts about what pandas eat and where they live. You may need to look in still other books to find all the information you need.

After Reading

Before you finish reading, think about what you learned. Ask yourself questions.

- Can I answer all of my purpose questions?
- Do I understand what I read?
- Can I explain the information in my own words?
- Have I kept track of the different books I used?

If you can't answer these questions, you might need to reread. It is normal to reread when you are using information books.

If you use more than one book, keep a list of the titles and the authors. You might need to look at them again or tell your teacher where you found the information. Create a list like this one below.

Title and Author List

<u>Giant Pandas</u> by Patricia A. Fink Martin

<u>Giant Pandas: Gifts from China</u> by Allan Fowler

Summing Up

- Be sure you understand the assignment and what information you need to find.
- Preview information books before reading. Decide which ones will be useful.
- Use Summary Notes to keep track of information.
- You may need to use more than one book to find all of the information you need.
- Keep track of the titles and authors of the books you use.

Information

173

Focus on a Website

The Internet is an amazing source of information. With one click of the mouse, you can learn about spaceships, lions, or skateboarding. That's the great thing about the Internet.

What is not so great about the Internet is that it's easy to get lost. There are millions of websites. Each one is full of words and pictures. If you try to read everything that seems interesting, you'll have a hard time finding what you need. Use the reading process to help you with websites.

Goals

Here you'll learn how to:

✔ use the reading process with a website

✔ keep track of and evaluate the information you find on the Internet

Before Reading

The World Wide Web is a great place to learn, but it is huge! This is why it's important for you to know what you're looking for when you start out.

Have a Clear Purpose

Setting a purpose first will make it easier for you to find the information you need. To set your purpose, ask yourself, "What do I want to find out?"

My purpose is

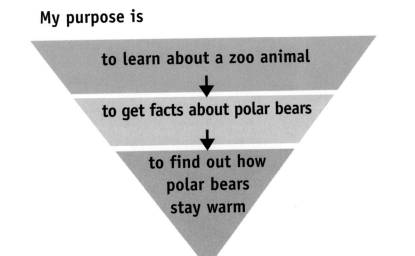

to learn about a zoo animal

↓

to get facts about polar bears

↓

to find out how polar bears stay warm

The last purpose is the best. It's the most specific.

Write your purpose question on a note card. Then you can take it with you to the computer.

How do polar bears stay warm?

Information

175

Preview the Website

Next, find a site that you think has the information you want. Let's say you decide to look at the website of the San Diego Zoo. Once you log on to the website, do a quick preview. Look for information about your specific subject—polar bears.

Sometimes it can take a little time to find what you're looking for. For instance, you don't see anything about polar bears, do you? Be patient. Look under "Animal Categories." Then, if you click on "Mammal," you'll find a page about polar bears.

During Reading

When you read a website, pay attention to the words and the graphics.

Stay on Track

Keep your purpose question in front of you as you read the website. There can be a lot to look at and read on the screen. You may find all sorts of interesting information. But stay on track. If you need facts on how polar bears stay warm, look for them. Look at the headings to find what you need.

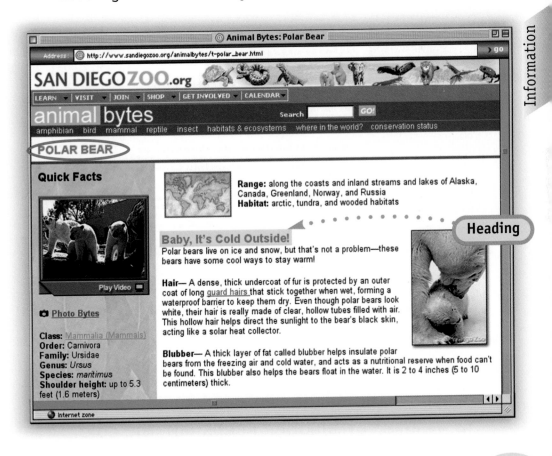

■ Information

Write Notes

Write down the important information you find. Start by listing the website address. That way you can find your way back to the website again. Make Summary Notes to help you remember what you learned.

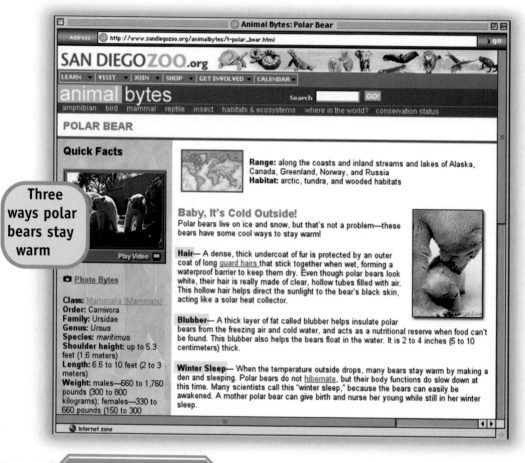

Three ways polar bears stay warm

Address: http://www.sandiegozoo.org/animalbytes/t-polar_bear.html

SAN DIEGO ZOO.org

LEARN ▼ | VISIT ▼ | JOIN ▼ | SHOP ▼ | GET INVOLVED ▼ | CALENDAR ▼

animal bytes   Search [   ] GO!

amphibian   bird   mammal   reptile   insect   habitats & ecosystems   where in the world?   conservation status

POLAR BEAR

Quick Facts

Play Video ■

📷 Photo Bytes

Class: Mammalia (Mammals)
Order: Carnivora
Family: Ursidae
Genus: Ursus
Species: maritimus
Shoulder height: up to 5.3 feet (1.6 meters)
Length: 6.6 to 10 feet (2 to 3 meters)
Weight: males—660 to 1,760 pounds (300 to 800 kilograms); females—330 to 660 pounds (150 to 300

Range: along the coasts and inland streams and lakes of Alaska, Canada, Greenland, Norway, and Russia
Habitat: arctic, tundra, and wooded habitats

Baby, It's Cold Outside!
Polar bears live on ice and snow, but that's not a problem—these bears have some cool ways to stay warm!

Hair— A dense, thick undercoat of fur is protected by an outer coat of long guard hairs that stick together when wet, forming a waterproof barrier to keep them dry. Even though polar bears look white, their hair is really made of clear, hollow tubes filled with air. This hollow hair helps direct the sunlight to the bear's black skin, acting like a solar heat collector.

Blubber— A thick layer of fat called blubber helps insulate polar bears from the freezing air and cold water, and acts as a nutritional reserve when food can't be found. This blubber also helps the bears float in the water. It is 2 to 4 inches (5 to 10 centimeters) thick.

Winter Sleep— When the temperature outside drops, many bears stay warm by making a den and sleeping. Polar bears do not hibernate, but their body functions do slow down at this time. Many scientists call this "winter sleep," because the bears can easily be awakened. A mother polar bear can give birth and nurse her young while still in her winter sleep.

🌐 Internet zone

Summary Notes

www.sandiegozoo.org/
Ways Polar Bears Stay Warm
   1. Their thick hair protects them.
   2. A layer of blubber keeps out the cold.
   3. They make a den and sleep in the winter.

Evaluate a Website

You can't trust everything you see, especially when it is on the Internet. Anybody can make a website. Try to evaluate every website you visit. That means you need to be sure that what it says is true and up-to-date.

You can use a Website Card to help you decide how good a site is.

◀ Website Card

NAME AND ADDRESS San Diego Zoo (www.sandiegozoo.org)
WHAT IT SAYS It gives facts about animals and shows pictures of them.
MY REACTION This seems very good. It has lots of information about zoo animals. It is easy to understand.

Information

Filling in a Website Card will help you decide how useful a site is. Some websites aren't very good. Make it a habit to keep cards on the good websites you visit.

After Reading

Be sure you have all the information you need from one website before you move on to another one. Take notes on the key facts. When you finish reading one web page, you can move to another.

Stop and read only if you see information about your reading purpose. Take notes on each good website you visit.

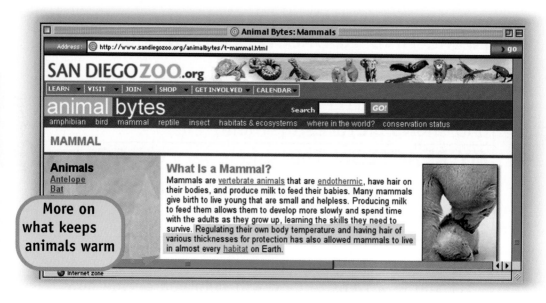

More on what keeps animals warm

Summing Up

- Write down your reading purpose question before you begin reading a website.
- Take notes on the exact information you find.
- Use a Website Card to evaluate a website.

Focus on Graphics

Think of graphics—tables, graphs, maps, diagrams—as word pictures. They show information in a way you can easily see, but you still have to read them.

You'll find graphics almost anywhere you look. They're in the newspaper, on your computer, and in your textbooks. Take some time here to learn how to read and respond to a graphic.

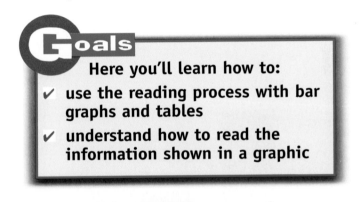

Goals

Here you'll learn how to:

✔ **use the reading process with bar graphs and tables**
✔ **understand how to read the information shown in a graphic**

Before Reading

In a graphic, the picture and words are equally important. Your job is to read and understand both of them.

Your purpose for reading a graphic usually stays the same, no matter what the graphic is about. Here are two good questions to ask when setting your purpose.

■ What is the graphic about?
■ What does it tell me?

During Reading

Usually it's not hard to tell what a graphic is about. First, read the title. Next, look at any labels, headings, and numbers. They will tell you a lot.

Read a Bar Graph

A bar graph compares two or more things at one point in time. The bars can go sideways or up and down. What do the bars in this graph compare?

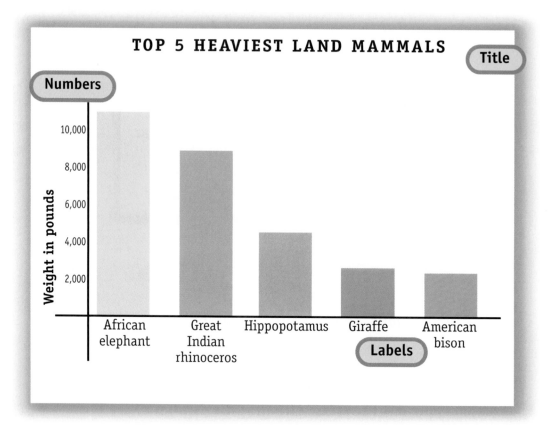

This bar graph compares the weights of the five heaviest land mammals. Usually the title will tell you exactly what a graphic is about.

How to Read a Bar Graph

Follow these steps when reading a bar graph.

1. Read the title. What is the subject of the graph?

2. Read the labels below each bar.

3. Notice the numbers on the left.

4. Draw conclusions about what the graph says.

Now read the land mammals graph again. Talk through what you see and read.

Think Aloud

This bar graph shows the weights of the five heaviest land mammals. The taller bars go with the heavier animals.

Information

Once you're clear on what the graphic shows, it's time to think about the information. Ask yourself, "What does this graphic tell me?" Your conclusion about this bar graph might be that the African elephant is the heaviest land mammal.

Read a Table

Tables contain information in *columns* (going down) and *rows* (going across). The table below gives facts about the five largest states.

Title

Column headings

THE 5 LARGEST STATES

State	Capital	Nickname	Area	Rank in Area
Alaska	Juneau	Last Frontier	587,878 sq. mi.	1
Texas	Austin	Lone Star State	266,874 sq. mi.	2
California	Sacramento	Golden State	158,648 sq. mi.	3
Montana	Helena	Treasure State	147,047 sq. mi.	4
New Mexico	Santa Fe	Land of Enchantment	121,599 sq. mi.	5

Row headings

Notice the different parts of the table above. It has a title, column headings, and row headings. Read them first to figure out what the table is about and how it is organized. Did you notice the states are listed in order of how big they are? Alaska comes first because it is ranked first in area.

184

How to Read a Table

Follow these steps when reading a table.

1. Read the title. Then read the column and row headings. Decide what the table is about.

2. Use your finger as a guide as you read each column or row.

3. Draw conclusions about what the table says.

Look again at the states table. Suppose you wanted to know how many square miles Montana covers.

First, go to Montana. Put your finger there or use a ruler. Second, read across the column headings until you find the one that says "Area." Third, read down that column to the Montana row. Now you know that Montana is 147,047 square miles.

Information

THE 5 LARGEST STATES

❷ State	Capital	Nickname	Area ❸	Rank in Area
Alaska	Juneau	Last Frontier	587,878 sq. mi.	1
Texas	Austin	Lone Star State	266,874 sq. mi.	2
California	Sacramento	Golden State	158,648 sq. mi.	3
❶ Montana	Helena	Treasure State	147,047 sq. mi.	4
New Mexico	Santa Fe	Land of Enchantment	121,599 sq. mi.	5

Draw Conclusions

After you understand what a graphic shows, you can begin to draw some conclusions. These are your own ideas about what the graphic means.

For example, take another look at the states table. Did you notice anything about where the five states are? They are all in the western part of the United States. So, one conclusion you might draw is that states are larger in the West than they are in the East.

How to Draw Conclusions

These questions can help you draw conclusions about a graphic. Make some notes in your notebook.

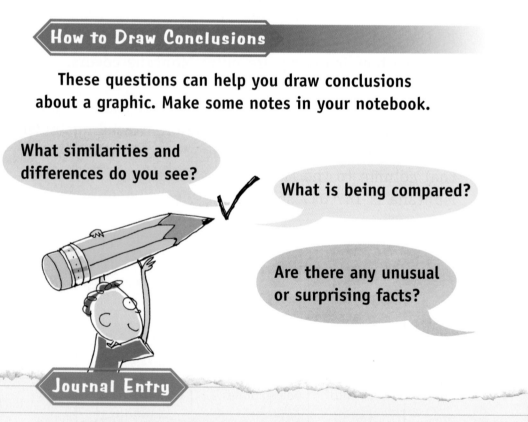

What similarities and differences do you see?

What is being compared?

Are there any unusual or surprising facts?

Journal Entry

I noticed that Alaska is more than twice the size of the next biggest state (Texas). I never knew that Alaska was so big!

After Reading

Different people will draw different conclusions from the same graphic. That's okay. When this happens, talk over the parts of the graphic and compare your ideas.

Ask questions about what is shown. Talking about what you see helps make reading graphics more interesting.

Try to connect what you're reading about to your own life. That will help you remember the information better.

Summing Up

■ **Bar graphs and tables are two common kinds of graphics.**

■ **When you read a graphic, ask yourself, "What is the graphic about? What does it tell me?"**

■ **Try to draw conclusions about what you see.**

■ **Make notes and talk about what the graphic shows.**

Information

Elements of Nonfiction

Information is all around you in newspapers, magazines, books, graphics, and websites. These are examples of nonfiction.

This part of the handbook explains some key terms. They are important to know when you read nonfiction. Use these terms to help you understand nonfiction.

Elements of Nonfiction

Bar Graph

A bar graph compares the numbers or amounts of things. The title usually tells what the graph is about.

EXAMPLE

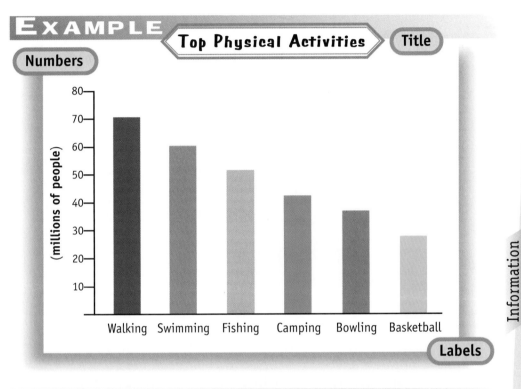

Top Physical Activities — **Title**

Numbers

(millions of people)

Walking Swimming Fishing Camping Bowling Basketball

Labels

Information

DESCRIPTION

This **bar graph** compares six popular activities. Use the numbers on the left to tell how many millions of people do each activity. You can compare numbers by measuring one bar against another. For example, you can tell by the length of the bars that more people go swimming than go bowling.

DEFINITION

A **bar graph** uses bars to show quantities, or how many. You can measure one bar against another to compare numbers or amounts.

Circle Graph

A circle graph, or pie chart, shows parts of a whole. Think of a round cake cut into slices. Each slice is a part of the whole.

EXAMPLE

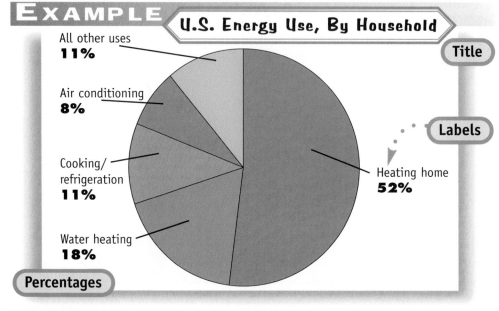

U.S. Energy Use, By Household

All other uses
11%

Air conditioning
8%

Cooking/
refrigeration
11%

Water heating
18%

Heating home
52%

Title

Labels

Percentages

DESCRIPTION

A **circle graph** shows how parts of something compare to one another and to the whole thing. From the title above, you can tell this circle graph shows different ways people use energy.

The labels tell you how we use energy. The size of the parts helps you compare how much energy is used in each way.

DEFINITION

A **circle graph** shows parts of a whole. The size of each part shows how much of the whole it is.

Details

Details are the words or phrases used to describe a person, place, thing, or idea. They make a piece of writing more real—and more interesting.

EXAMPLE

from *Eleanor Everywhere* by Monica Kulling

In 1929, the stock market crashed. Millions of Americans lost their jobs. They lost their farms. They lost their homes. They wandered from state to state looking for work. There was no unemployment insurance. There was no money for food. There was hunger. And there was sorrow.

The Great Depression, as it came to be called, would last for several years.

> Specific details

DESCRIPTION

Details give life to a description, support an argument, or explain an idea. In this example, the writer gives all kinds of details about the time period of the Great Depression. She tells how people lost their jobs and their homes. She says that people were hungry and sad. These details help you form a picture in your mind of what the author is describing.

DEFINITION

Details are short facts and descriptions that add life to a piece of writing.

Diagram

You see diagrams in your math, science, and history textbooks. You'll also see them in newspapers, magazine articles, and on the Internet.

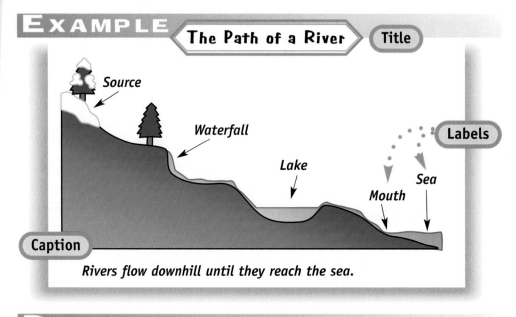

EXAMPLE

The Path of a River — Title

Source

Waterfall

Lake

Labels

Sea

Mouth

Caption

Rivers flow downhill until they reach the sea.

DESCRIPTION

A **diagram** is a drawing with labels. Its purpose is to show or explain something. A diagram usually includes labels that tell the names of parts.

To read a diagram, look first at the title. Then read each label and see what it's showing. Be sure to read the *caption*. It helps you understand what the diagram is about.

DEFINITION

A **diagram** is a picture with labels. It shows the shape, parts, or steps of something.

Email

Email is a kind of letter or message. The *e* in *email* stands for "electronic." Sending email is like mailing a letter, except it travels over the Internet.

EXAMPLE

Email address

Header

From: info@trentonzooinfo.org
To: steven_wells@trentonelementary.edu
Date: Thurs., Dec. 4, 2003 9:25 AM
Subject: Information on zoo programs

Body

Hi Steven,
Thanks for your email. I'm glad your class wants to visit our zoo. We have many programs for students. You can find information at our website: www.trentonzoo.org. Click on the red information box to find answers to all your questions.

Information

DESCRIPTION

Most **emails** that you receive will contain two basic parts: the *header* and the *body*. In the header, you'll see the email address of the person who sent the message. The header also shows your email address, the date, and the subject of the message. The body is the message itself.

DEFINITION

Email is electronic mail that travels over the Internet.

Encyclopedia

An encyclopedia gives information about many different topics.

EXAMPLE

from *The World Book Encyclopedia*

Entry word

Tepee, also spelled *tipi,* was the type of tent most commonly used by the Plains tribes of North American Indians. A tepee was made by stretching a buffalo-skin covering over poles. The poles were arranged in the shape of a cone. At the top, the ends of the poles crossed and stuck out of the covering. Two flap "ears" were opened at the top to let out smoke from the campfire. The tent was pegged to the ground all around the bottom. The front had a slit partly closed with wooden pins to form an entrance.

Detailed information

W. Roger Buffalohead

Author's name

DESCRIPTION

An **encyclopedia** is a set of books (or a CD) with articles on all kinds of topics. The topic of the article above is tepees. The entry word, or topic, is in boldface. The articles are in alphabetical order.

DEFINITION

An **encyclopedia** is a collection of articles, in alphabetical order, on many different topics.

Fact and Opinion

In nonfiction, facts and opinions are often mixed together. They can be in the same paragraph—or even in the same sentence. Can you find them in this paragraph?

EXAMPLE from *Amazing Flying Machines* by Robin Kerrod

The helicopter is a most remarkable flying machine. Not only can it fly forward, but it can fly sideways and backward too. It can hover in the air like a hawk, and it takes off and lands straight up and down.

Opinion

Facts

DESCRIPTION

A **fact** is something that can be proved. An **opinion** is someone's personal belief. This example opens with an opinion: helicopters are remarkable. After that, the author supports the opinion with a series of facts.

In the paragraph above, you learn how helicopters fly, take off, and land. You can prove that a helicopter is able to do all of these things. You can't prove that a helicopter is remarkable. Even though you can't prove an opinion, you should support it with facts and details.

DEFINITION

A **fact** is something that can be proved to be true. An **opinion** is a belief or feeling about a subject.

Information

Line Graph

A line graph is a kind of picture. It shows how something changes over time or how one thing compares to another.

EXAMPLE

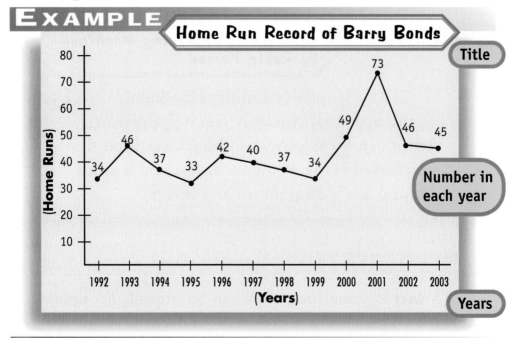

Home Run Record of Barry Bonds — Title

Number in each year

Years

DESCRIPTION

This **line graph** shows the number of home runs Barry Bonds has hit since 1992. The bottom of the graph shows the time, or years. The left side shows the subject, home runs.

A steep line means a strong, fast change. A flat line means the change was less strong and fast. For instance, look at the line between the last two numbers on the right. It is almost flat. That's because there's hardly any change between the number of home runs Bonds hit in 2002 and 2003.

DEFINITION

A **line graph** shows changes over time.

Main Idea

The main idea of a paragraph or article is the author's key message. It is the most important idea.

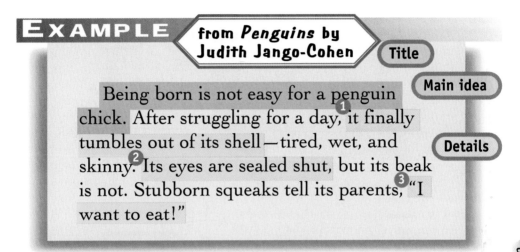

EXAMPLE

from *Penguins* by Judith Jango-Cohen

Title

Main idea

Being born is not easy for a penguin chick. After struggling for a day, it finally tumbles out of its shell—tired, wet, and skinny. Its eyes are sealed shut, but its beak is not. Stubborn squeaks tell its parents, "I want to eat!"

Details

DESCRIPTION

The **main idea** is what the author wants you to remember most. The subject in the example above is a penguin baby. The main idea is that being born is not easy for a penguin baby. The main idea is different from the subject. Notice how the author supports the main idea with three strong details.

Main ideas can come at the beginning, middle, or end. Sometimes the main idea is stated clearly, as in this example. Other times, you need to figure it out, or infer it, on your own.

DEFINITION

The **main idea** is the most important point the author wants to make.

Information

Map

Maps show information about places and key features of places.

EXAMPLE

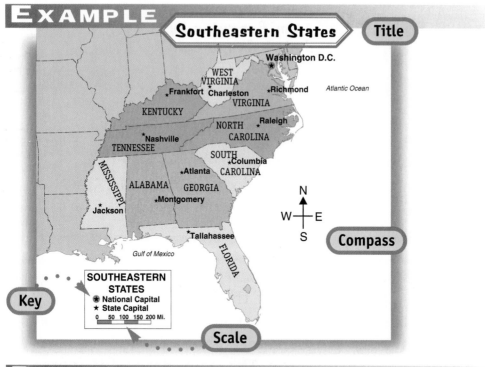

Southeastern States — Title

Washington D.C.
WEST VIRGINIA
Frankfort Charleston Richmond   Atlantic Ocean
KENTUCKY   VIRGINIA
                NORTH Raleigh
                CAROLINA
Nashville
TENNESSEE
                SOUTH
                    Columbia
            Atlanta CAROLINA
MISSISSIPPI ALABAMA GEORGIA
        Montgomery
Jackson
                                N
                            W ┼ E   Compass
                                S
            Tallahassee
    Gulf of Mexico   FLORIDA

Key

SOUTHEASTERN STATES
✹ National Capital
★ State Capital
0 50 100 150 200 Mi.

Scale

DESCRIPTION

The title of this **map** tells its subject: states in the southeastern United States. The *key*, or *legend*, contains symbols that help you understand what's shown. Here the stars mark the states' capital cities. The *compass* shows direction (north, south, east, and west). The *scale* helps you measure how far it is between places.

DEFINITION

Maps are pictures of places. They tell you where something is.

Table

A table is a kind of chart. It can organize a lot of facts in a small space. The purpose of a table is to show how different kinds of information fit together.

EXAMPLE

Countries — Title — Column headings

Countries

Name	Capital City	Main Language	Population (millions of people)
Japan	Tokyo	Japanese	127
India	New Delhi	Hindi	1,030
China	Beijing	Chinese	1,273
Australia	Canberra	English	19
United States	Washington, D.C.	English	281

Row headings

DESCRIPTION

A **table** has *rows* (going across) and *columns* (going down). It can show all types of information, including numbers, names, and dates. This table compares some facts about five countries.

Read all the headings. Sometimes you will read across a row first. Other times you might start by looking at the information in a column.

DEFINITION

A **table** is a list of facts that are arranged in columns and rows.

Information

Timeline

A timeline shows important events and the order in which they happened.

EXAMPLE

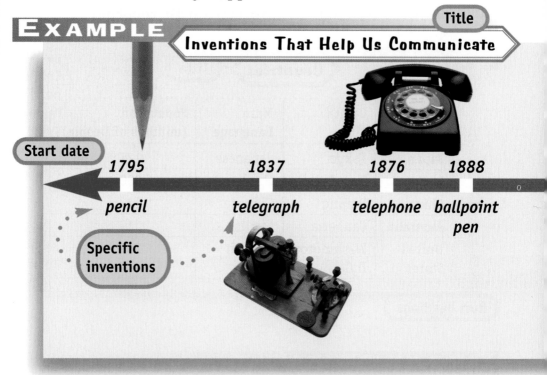

Title

Inventions That Help Us Communicate

Start date

1795   1837   1876   1888

pencil   telegraph   telephone ballpoint
                                          pen

Specific
inventions

DESCRIPTION

On a **timeline,** there is always a *start date* (1795 in this timeline) and an *end date* (1994). The words above or below the timeline explain what happened on those dates.

Timelines show the order of events. In the timeline above, the pencil was invented first, then the telegraph, then later the telephone, and so on. Timelines are especially useful when you read history or biographies.

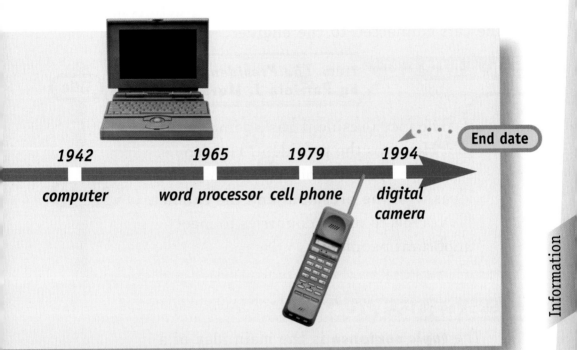

1942   1965   1979   1994   End date

computer   word processor cell phone   digital
                                          camera

DEFINITION

A **timeline** shows events in time order—what
happened first, what happened next, and so on.
A timeline can help you explore how the events
are related.

Topic Sentence and Supporting Details

A paragraph is sort of like a train. The topic sentence is the engine. The supporting details are the cars connected to the engine.

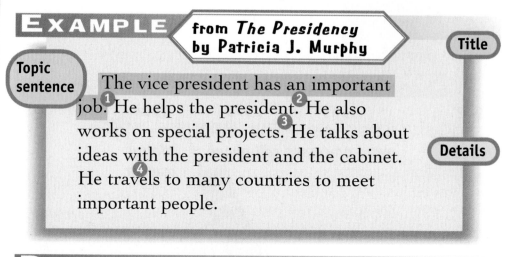

EXAMPLE from *The Presidency* by Patricia J. Murphy

Title

Topic sentence

The vice president has an important job. He helps the president. He also works on special projects. He talks about ideas with the president and the cabinet. He travels to many countries to meet important people.

Details

DESCRIPTION

The **topic sentence** is the main idea of a paragraph. It usually comes at the beginning of the paragraph.

A topic sentence can tell a fact. Or, it can give an opinion. The topic sentence in the example above gives an opinion. It says that the vice president's job is important.

In a good paragraph, all of the sentences relate to the topic sentence. These other sentences contain **supporting details.** They make it easier for you to understand the topic sentence.

Organization of the Paragraph

TOPIC SENTENCE The vice president has an important job.			
DETAIL 1 He helps the president.	**DETAIL 2** He works on special projects.	**DETAIL 3** He talks about ideas with the president and the cabinet.	**DETAIL 4** He travels to other countries and meets important people.

Note how each detail in the example paragraph relates to the topic sentence. Each one helps you understand why the vice president is important. If a topic sentence states an opinion, the supporting details should explain why the opinion is true.

DEFINITION

A **topic sentence** tells the main idea of the paragraph. It tells what the paragraph is about. The **supporting details** help explain the topic sentence. They give examples and facts to show that the topic sentence is true.

Information

Website

A website is a page or group of pages that are on the World Wide Web. Each website has its own address on the Internet.

EXAMPLE

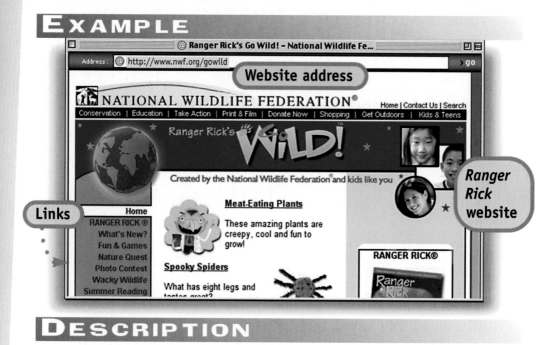

DESCRIPTION

Some **websites** are for learning, and some are for fun. The *Ranger Rick* site above combines both fun and learning. It mixes art, words, and other cool features.

A website can have one page or thousands of them. In most cases, the *home page,* or opening page of the site, will be your first stop. It shows what's on the website. From it, you can *link,* or connect, to other pages on the website.

DEFINITION

A **website** is a page or group of pages that are linked together on the World Wide Web.

World Wide Web

The World Wide Web is the biggest library you can imagine. With a computer, you can find information about almost anything on the World Wide Web.

EXAMPLE

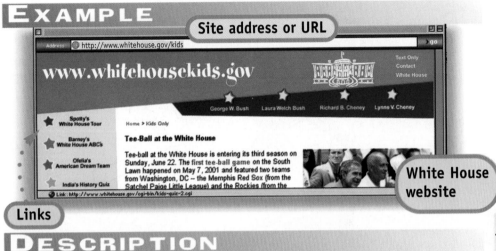

Site address or URL

Links

White House website

DESCRIPTION

The **World Wide Web** links computers all over the world that can "talk" to each other. What allows them to talk is a kind of electronic highway known as the *Internet*.

Every website has its own address. This address is called a *URL* (uniform resource locator). To go to a website, type in the address. Then press the "enter" or "return" key.

Did you notice the stars on the White House website? They show *links*. Clicking on one of these takes you to information about other topics.

DEFINITION

The **World Wide Web** is a system of computers that share information.

Information

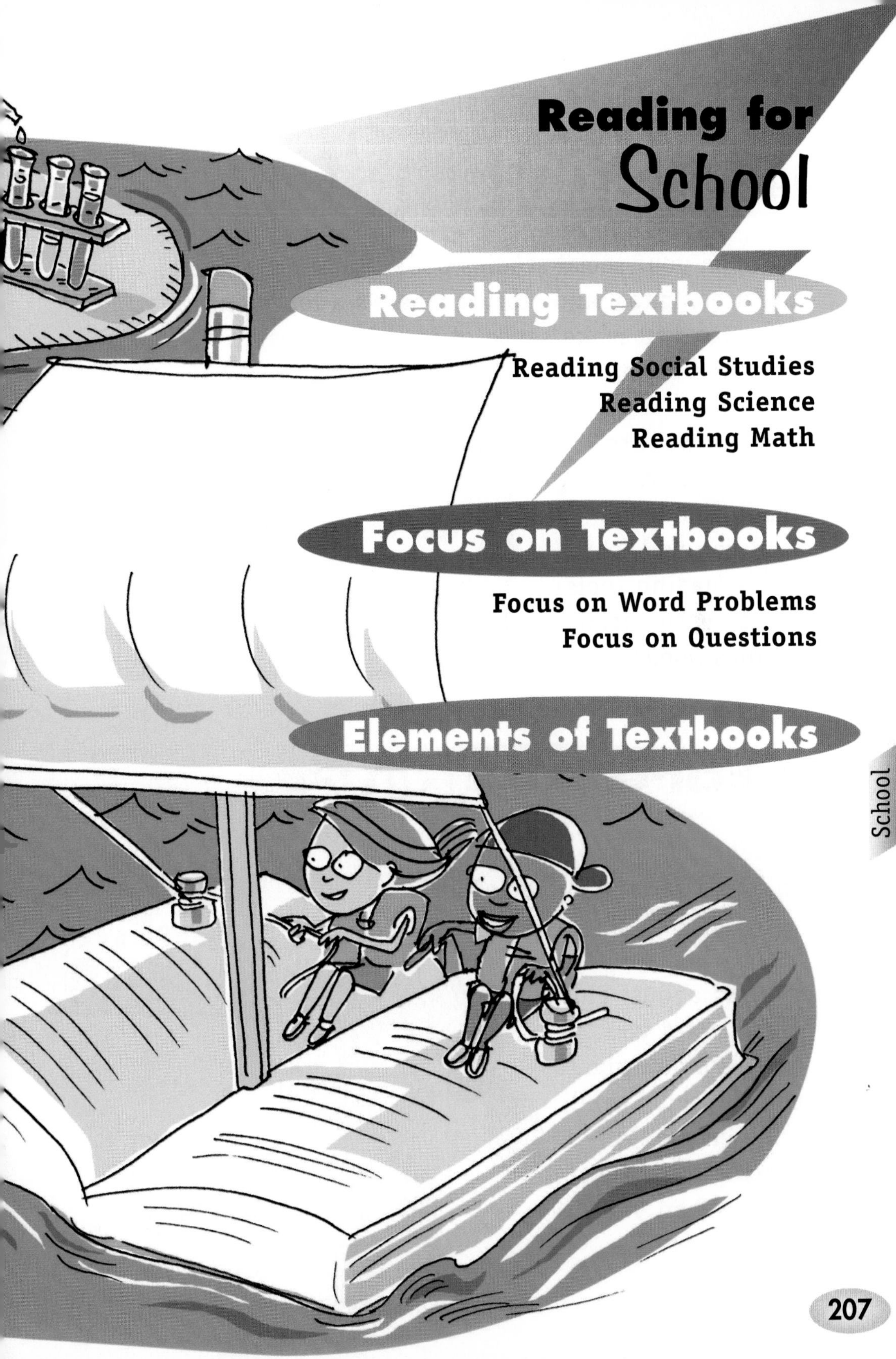

Reading for School

Reading Textbooks

Reading Social Studies
Reading Science
Reading Math

Focus on Textbooks

Focus on Word Problems
Focus on Questions

Elements of Textbooks

Reading Social Studies

Open your social studies book. What do you see? It has pictures, maps, and stories. There's a lot of information. How can you make sense of it all? It's easy if you go one step at a time.

Here we'll teach you to use the reading process. And you will learn some reading tools to use with social studies books.

Goals

Here you'll learn how to:

✔ **read and understand** social studies textbooks

✔ **practice the strategy of** using graphic organizers

Before Reading

Take a few minutes to look over a chapter before you start reading. Try to learn what you're reading about. Think about what you already know about the subject. Spend a few moments looking over the pages. Then you're ready to start.

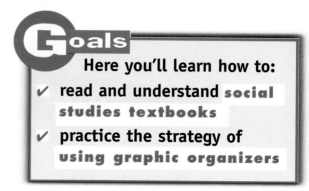

A Set a Purpose

At school, you have textbooks. More and more often, your teacher will assign pages in them to read. You need to be ready.

Suppose you had to read a social studies chapter called "A Capital for the U.S.A." It is about how Washington, D.C., became the capital city. What questions would you need to ask yourself?

- **How did Washington, D.C., become the country's capital?**
- **Why is this information important to me?**

B Preview

When you preview a textbook chapter, take a quick look at each page. Run your finger down the center of each page. Read the headings and words in boldface. Let your eyes stop on words or pictures that stand out.

School

Look for the items on the checklist below. Touch each checklist item as you find it.

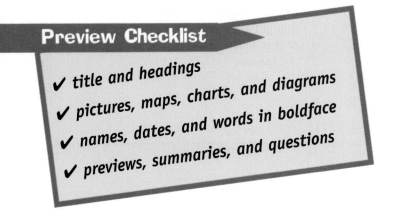

Preview Checklist

✔ title and headings
✔ pictures, maps, charts, and diagrams
✔ names, dates, and words in boldface
✔ previews, summaries, and questions

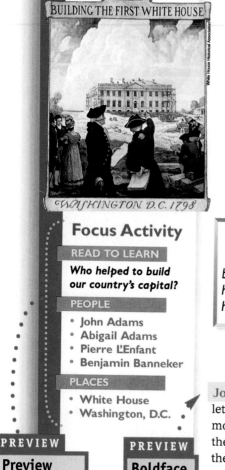

BUILDING THE FIRST WHITE HOUSE

WASHINGTON D.C. 1798

Focus Activity

READ TO LEARN

Who helped to build our country's capital?

PEOPLE

- John Adams
- Abigail Adams
- Pierre L'Enfant
- Benjamin Banneker

PLACES

- White House
- Washington, D.C.

PREVIEW

Preview information

PREVIEW

Boldface terms

A Capital for the U.S.A.

PREVIEW

Title

Read Aloud

"I pray heaven to bestow [give] the best of blessings on this house and on all that shall hereafter inhabit [live in] it. May none but honest and wise men ever rule under this roof."

PREVIEW

Heading

A Capital Is Needed

The words above were written by President John Adams in 1800. They were written in a letter to his wife, Abigail, the day after he moved into the White House. John Adams was the second President of the United States and the first President to live in the White House.

Just a few years earlier, the leaders of the United States had trouble deciding where to build a capital city for the new country.

Thomas Jefferson, who was from the South, thought the capital should be in one of the southern states. Leaders from the North thought Boston or New York would be a good choice. Others thought Philadelphia should be the capital.

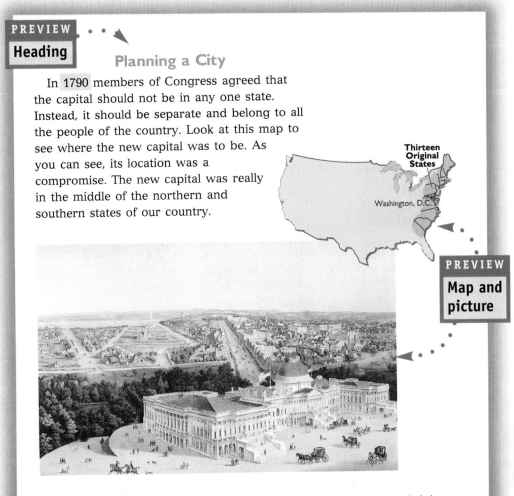

PREVIEW

Heading

Planning a City

In 1790 members of Congress agreed that the capital should not be in any one state. Instead, it should be separate and belong to all the people of the country. Look at this map to see where the new capital was to be. As you can see, its location was a compromise. The new capital was really in the middle of the northern and southern states of our country.

Thirteen Original States

Washington, D.C.

PREVIEW

Map and picture

School

President Washington hired a French builder named Pierre L'Enfant (pee AIR lah FAHN) to draw up plans for the new capital.

L'Enfant came to America in 1777. He was in the army and fought for the colonists during the American Revolution. L'Enfant designed a grand city, with wide streets and magnificent buildings. But he didn't get along with other planners. He left in the middle of the planning. And he took his plans with him!

Here is our capital city long ago. The new streets and buildings were built on land that once was a forest.

PREVIEW

Names and dates

PREVIEW
Heading

PREVIEW
Boldface terms

Life in the New Capital

Luckily, a man named Benjamin Banneker (BAN ih kur) had a good memory. Banneker had been one of L'Enfant's assistants. He had also worked hard on the plans for the new city. He sat down with other planners. Together they redrew L'Enfant's plans.

The new capital was named after George Washington. It was called Washington, D.C. The *D.C.* stands for District of Columbia.

The first building to be built in the new capital was the White House. In 1800 Abigail Adams was eager to start life in the new house. In her letters to her sister Mary, Abigail described life in the new capital. Read the letter below. What does it tell you about living in Washington, D.C., in 1800?

Benjamin Banneker was honored on a United States stamp.

PREVIEW
Pictures

PREVIEW
Names and dates

MANY VOICES
PRIMARY SOURCE

Letter written by Abigail Adams in 1800.

M**Y DEAR SISTER:**

I expected to find it a new country, with scattered houses over a space of ten miles, and trees and stumps in plenty with a castle of a house. I found the President's House is in a beautiful situation in front of which is the Potomac [River]. . . . The country around is romantic but wild, a wilderness at present.

WHY IT MATTERS

Abigail Adams's letters give us a look into the past. If she could have looked into the future, she might have been very surprised. There have been many changes to the White House since she lived there. Every year has also brought other changes to our country's capital. In the next lesson you will look at Washington, D.C., today.

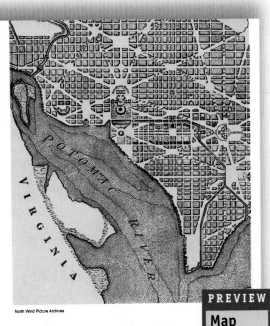

Early plans for Washington, D.C., included wide streets and open areas.

North Wind Picture Archives

PREVIEW

Summary

PREVIEW

Map

✓ Reviewing Facts and Ideas

MAIN IDEAS

- John Adams was the second President of the United States. In 1800 he and his wife Abigail became the first people to live in the newly built White House.

- The leaders of the country compromised and chose Washington, D.C., as the location for the capital. The new capital city would be in the middle of the country and would not be part of any one state.

- Pierre L'Enfant drew up the first plans for the capital. When he left in the middle of planning, Benjamin Banneker helped to redraw the plans.

THINK ABOUT IT

1. Why did people disagree about where the new capital should be? How did they compromise?

2. **FOCUS** Who helped to build our country's capital?

3. **THINKING SKILL** Suppose you had to choose a location for the United States capital today. Where should it be? How would you *decide*?

4. **GEOGRAPHY** Leaders chose to build the new city along the Potomac River. Most cities at that time were located on or near rivers. Why do you think that was so?

School

PREVIEW

Questions

C Plan

What did you see on your preview? Maybe you picked up on these important details.

- The capital of the United States is Washington, D.C.
- People had trouble deciding where the capital city should be.
- Lots of people worked to plan the city.

Reading Strategy: ## Using Graphic Organizers

Once you have an idea of what the reading is about, choose a reading strategy to use. Using graphic organizers will help you keep track of key details in a social studies text. Graphic organizers are word pictures, such as charts, lists, and pictures. Use them to help you understand and remember what you've read.

A K-W-L Chart can help you connect what you already know about a subject with new information. It also can help you organize the questions you want to answer.

K-W-L Chart

WHAT I KNOW	WHAT I WANT TO KNOW	WHAT I LEARNED

Jot down what you already know here.

Write your questions here.

Write answers to your questions here.

During Reading

Active readers read slowly and carefully, but they also read with a specific purpose.

D Read with a Purpose

Remember your purpose. You are reading to find out what you can about how Washington, D.C., became the capital. Start by making notes on your K-W-L Chart. Here is an example.

TOOLS FOR SOCIAL STUDIES

✔ K-W-L Chart
✔ Timeline
✔ Web

K-W-L Chart

WHAT I KNOW	WHAT I WANT TO KNOW	WHAT I LEARNED
• Washington, D.C., is not in any state. • The White House is there.	• Why was Washington, D.C., chosen? • Who decided what the city should be like?	

Now go back to pages 210–213 and read "A Capital for the U.S.A."

Read for Names, Dates, and Events

Most social studies books are full of names, dates, and events. As you read, pay attention to them. Ask yourself, "*What* event does the chapter describe? *Who* was involved in the event? *When* did it take place?"

Taking notes on the people and events will help you remember the important parts. Two tools that work well for social studies notes are Webs and Timelines. A Web helps you keep related ideas together.

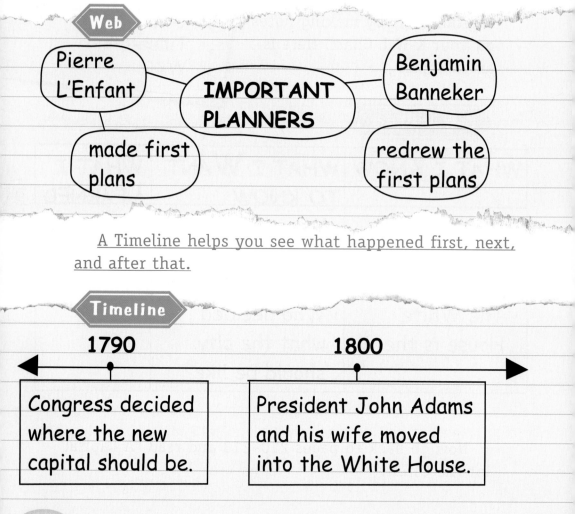

Web

Pierre L'Enfant — IMPORTANT PLANNERS — Benjamin Banneker

Pierre L'Enfant — made first plans

Benjamin Banneker — redrew the first plans

A Timeline helps you see what happened first, next, and after that.

Timeline

1790 — Congress decided where the new capital should be.

1800 — President John Adams and his wife moved into the White House.

Keep Track of Different Topics

Most social studies chapters tell about one main topic and two or more smaller topics. Pay attention to the headings in a chapter. They will help you figure out how the chapter is organized. Usually the chapter title tells you the main topic. The headings tell you what smaller topics are covered. "A Capital for the U.S.A." has three headings.

Web

A Capital Is Needed

"A CAPITAL FOR THE U.S.A."

Life in the New Capital

Main topic

Planning a City

Smaller topics

School

A Web can also keep track of the details of a topic. Read what's under a heading. Then write the most important details on the spokes of the Web.

Web

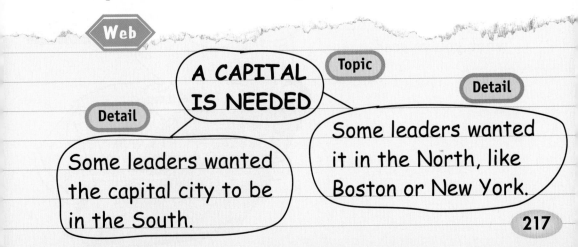

A CAPITAL IS NEEDED

Topic

Detail

Detail

Some leaders wanted the capital city to be in the South.

Some leaders wanted it in the North, like Boston or New York.

217

E Connect

When you read, think about why the information is important to you. Consider how it makes you feel. Try to connect to the topic. It can keep you interested in what you're reading and help you understand more.

Here are notes made after reading one part of "A Capital for the U.S.A."

- Pierre L'Enfant drew up the first plans for the capital. When he left in the middle of planning, Benjamin Banneker helped to redraw the plans.

People were probably mad at L'Enfant when he left. I would have been.

After Reading

You've finally finished reading the chapter. But wait! Before you close your book, take the time to think about what you've read.

F Pause and Reflect

Now reflect on what you read. Ask yourself some questions to check your understanding.

- **Have I met my purpose?**
- **Can I name key people, dates, events, and places?**
- **Do I understand everything I read?**

If you can't answer "yes" to these questions, then you need to do some rereading.

G Reread

Even the best readers need to reread sometimes. Rereading is easier than reading. On a second reading, you can read more smoothly and understand more.

Sometimes you'll want to reread a chapter word for word. You would do this, for example, if you didn't understand the main idea of the chapter. Other times, you'll only need to reread certain parts. You might need to answer a specific question like this.

School

> **1.** Why did people disagree about where the new capital should be? How did they compromise?

You would need to find the part that talks about why people disagreed. Look quickly through the chapter for the words *disagree, capital,* and *compromise.* Then read for the answer.

H Remember

A big part of learning is remembering what you read. So, you need to find a way to recall key details.

Talk about what you read with a friend. Write information in your own words. Here your K-W-L Chart can help. After you read, write important facts you learned in the "L" column of the chart.

K-W-L Chart

WHAT I KNOW	WHAT I WANT TO KNOW	WHAT I LEARNED
• Washington, D.C., is not in any state. • The White House is there.	• Why was Washington, D.C., chosen? • Who decided what the city should be like?	• People wanted the new capital to be in the middle of the northern and southern states. • Pierre L'Enfant and Benjamin Banneker helped plan the city. • The D.C. stands for District of Columbia.

ⓢumming Up

The reading process makes it easier for you to get more from a social studies text. The strategy of **using graphic organizers** can help you keep track of key information. Three note-taking tools work well with social studies:

- K-W-L Chart
- Web
- Timeline

School

Reading Science

Have you ever wondered where waves come from? Do you know why bears sleep through the winter?

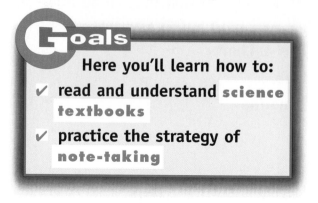

Goals

Here you'll learn how to:

✔ **read and understand** `science textbooks`

✔ **practice the strategy of** `note-taking`

People everywhere ask questions about nature and their world. To find answers, you can open a science book and begin reading.

Before Reading

Science has its own language. Many of the words you read in a science textbook will be new to you. Some of the information will also be new to you. A lot of science reading explains why and how things happen.

A Set a Purpose

You need to think about your purpose before reading science. Turn the title of the chapter into a *what, how,* or *why* question.

For example, here are two purpose questions you might ask for a chapter called "How Plants Make Food."

- **How do plants make food?**
- **What do they do with the food they make?**

B Preview

Look for key terms as you preview. Try also to get a sense of what you will learn from the reading. In your preview, pay attention to the items on this checklist:

Preview Checklist

✔ title and headings
✔ boldface terms
✔ previews and review questions
✔ photos, maps, and diagrams

School

How Plants Make Food

Making Food

Like other animals, you cannot make food in your body. You must get your food by eating. Plants, however, can make their own food. This food-making process is called **photosynthesis** (foht•oh•SIN•thuh•sis). A process is a way of doing something.

The leaves of most plants are green. Plants get their green color from **chlorophyll** (KLAWR•uh•fil). Chlorophyll helps the plant use energy from the sun to make food. Plants need light to make food. They also need water and carbon dioxide. Carbon dioxide is a gas in the air.

FIND OUT

- how plants make their own food
- why plants need chlorophyll to make their food

VOCABULARY

photosynthesis
chlorophyll

The sun provides light energy to plants.

◄ A plant that gets enough light (and soil and water) grows into a healthy plant.

▲ A plant that does not get enough light does not grow well, even though it has soil and water. It may die.

THE INSIDE STORY

Photosynthesis

During photosynthesis, a plant takes in sunlight, water, and carbon dioxide. The chlorophyll in the leaves lets the plant use these things to make food. The plant makes sugar and gives off oxygen.

Sunlight

Carbon dioxide

Chlorophyll

Oxygen

Water

School

During photosynthesis, water and carbon dioxide are used by the plant to make food. Sunlight provides the energy needed for this to happen. The food the plant makes is a kind of sugar. The plant uses some of the sugar right away and stores the rest.

During photosynthesis, plants also make oxygen. The oxygen is given off into the air through the plant's leaves. The bubbles you observed in the investigation were oxygen given off by the leaves into the water.

✓ **Name four things plants need for photosynthesis.**

PREVIEW

Review question

225

PREVIEW

Heading

How Plants Use Food

Plants use some of the food they make to grow larger. They also use it to make seeds. Some plants store food in their stems and roots so they can use it later. Other plants store sugar in fruits. This makes the fruit tasty to animals, who eat it and spread the seeds.

The stems, leaves, roots, seeds, fruits, and even flowers of plants are used as food by people and other animals.

PREVIEW

Review question

▲ Bananas grow in bunches called hands.

✔ **What are three ways plants use the food they make?**

◀ People eat the red fruit of the strawberry plant.

PREVIEW

Photos

◀ The stalks of celery plants contain fiber and water.

A potato is an underground stem that stores food made by the potato plant. ▼

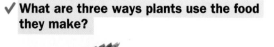

▲ When you break open a pea pod you can see the pea seeds inside.

Summary

Photosynthesis is the process plants use to make their own food. Plants need chlorophyll, light, carbon dioxide, and water for photosynthesis. The sun provides the light energy that plants need to make food. Plants use the food they make to grow bigger and to make seeds. They store some of their food in roots, stems, and fruits. People and other animals eat many different plant parts.

Review

1. Describe what happens during photosynthesis.
2. Why are plants green?
3. How does chlorophyll help in photosynthesis?
4. **Critical Thinking** How does photosynthesis help make the food people and other animals eat?
5. **Test Prep** What do plants give off during photosynthesis?
   A carbon dioxide
   B water
   C oxygen
   D light

LINKS

MATH LINK

Make a Graph Make a list of 20 foods you eat that come from plants. Identify how many of these foods come from roots, stems, leaves, fruits, seeds, and flowers. Make a bar graph from your list.

WRITING LINK

Informative Writing— Explanation Plants are like food factories. Use what you know about photosynthesis to write a paragraph for your teacher that explains how a plant is like a factory.

LANGUAGE ARTS LINK

Putting It Together The word *photosynthesis* is made up of the words *photo* and *synthesis*. Use a dictionary to find out what these words mean.

TECHNOLOGY LINK

To learn more about how people use the food that plants store, watch *Grocery Garden* on the **Science Newsroom Video.**

School

Plan

You probably noticed lots of things during your preview. Which of these facts did you see?

- Plants make food during photosynthesis.
- They have chlorophyll.
- Animals eat the food plants make.

You may not have seen everything on this list. Different readers notice different things during a preview. But a preview should give everyone an idea of the subject.

Reading Strategy: Note-taking

Note-taking is a good strategy to use with science. It helps you understand and remember what you have read.

You can take notes in a few different ways. Because science is about *how* and *why*, Process Notes are a good choice. Process Notes help you keep track of steps, stages, or events.

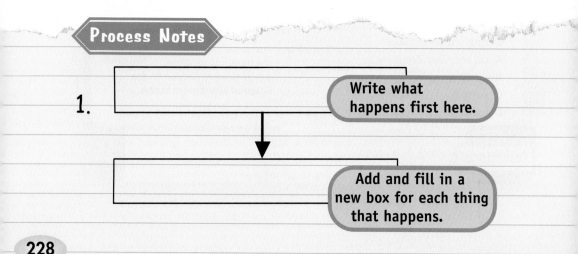

Process Notes

1.

Write what happens first here.

Add and fill in a new box for each thing that happens.

During Reading

After you plan which strategy to use, start your slow and careful reading of "How Plants Make Food."

D Read with a Purpose

Have a pen or pencil and some paper handy as you read. You should take notes as you go along.

Understand a Process

Scientists often want to explain the steps in a process. This chapter, for instance, explains photosynthesis, or the process of how plants make food. Here is an example of Process Notes. It tells how the process of photosynthesis happens.

Process Notes

PHOTOSYNTHESIS

School

1. The plant takes in sunlight, water, and carbon dioxide.

   ▼

2. Chlorophyll helps the plant use these to make food.

   ▼

3. The plant makes sugar and gives off oxygen.

Understand Cause and Effect

Scientists also think about cause and effect. A *cause* is why something happens. An *effect* is what happens as a result. A Cause-Effect Organizer is a good tool to use when you want to show *why* something happened.

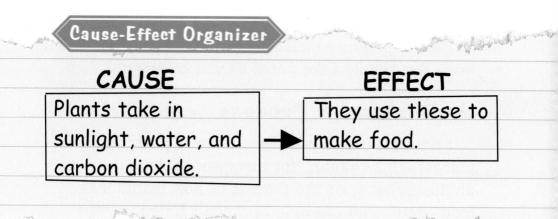

Cause-Effect Organizer

CAUSE	EFFECT
Plants take in sunlight, water, and carbon dioxide.	They use these to make food.

The Cause-Effect Organizers you make will not all look the same. Sometimes there may be more than one cause or effect. For instance, here is an organizer that shows two effects.

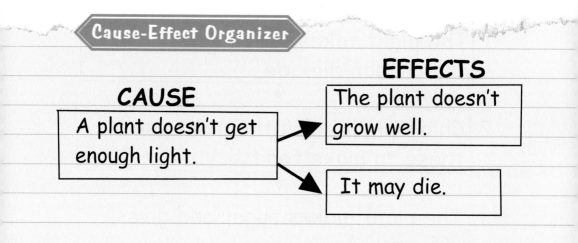

Cause-Effect Organizer

EFFECTS

CAUSE

A plant doesn't get enough light.

The plant doesn't grow well.

It may die.

E Connect

Science is easier to read and more interesting if you connect it to your own life. As you read, ask yourself, "What does this information have to do with me?"

> The stems, leaves, roots, seeds, fruits, and even flowers of plants are used as food by people and other animals.

Squirrels ate the flowers my mom planted.

With everything you read, try to see how it fits in with your life.

After Reading

After you finish reading, think about what you learned.

F Pause and Reflect

Look back over the lesson. Ask yourself how well you've understood what you read. Can you answer "yes" to questions like these?

- **Do I understand what the main topics are?**
- **Can I explain the key terms and diagrams?**
- **Can I answer the review questions?**

School

G Reread

If the chapter you read was difficult, you might need to reread all of it again. Do this, for example, if you're not clear about how plants make food.

Other times, you might need to reread only a small part. For example, you might want to reread so you can answer this review question.

> ✔ **What are three ways plants use the food they make?**

You need to find the part of the chapter that tells about ways plants use food. That's not too hard. There's a heading about exactly this topic.

Three ways plants use food

How Plants Use Food

Plants use some of the food they ① make to grow larger. They also use it ② to make seeds. Some plants store ③ food in their stems and roots so they can use it later. Other plants store sugar in fruits. This makes the fruit tasty to animals, who eat it and spread the seeds.

You can find the specific information you need when you take the time to reread.

H Remember

How can you remember everything you've read in science? People forget some of the things they have heard or read. But that's why you take notes.

Look again at the notes you made. Then try writing down some of the other information you learned.

■ Make flashcards with science terms and their meanings.
■ Write a quick list of three to five facts you learned.

Summing Up

When you read science, use the strategy of **note-taking.** It can help you learn and remember important facts. Two tools are especially useful for keeping track of science information:

- **Process Notes**
- **Cause-Effect Organizer**

School

Reading Math

To do well in math, you have to be a good reader. That might sound strange, but think about it. Your textbook is the best tool you have for learning math. It has explanations, examples, and practice problems. All of these things can make it easier for you to understand math.

But many students have trouble reading their math book. This makes math harder for them to learn. You can avoid this problem by using the reading process with your math textbook.

Goals

Here you'll learn how to:

✔ **read a math book for key information**

✔ **use the strategy of visualizing and thinking aloud to solve problems**

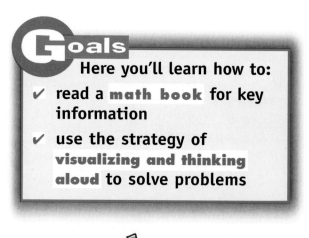

Before Reading

Compared to most books, a math textbook doesn't have many words. In math books, every word on a page counts. You need to take your time when reading math.

A Set a Purpose

First, understand your purpose for reading. You can ask yourself these two questions.

- **What is the main topic of this lesson?**
- **How do I solve these kinds of problems?**

B Preview

Next, preview the lesson you're about to read. Let your eyes move down each page. Look for the items on this Preview Checklist:

School

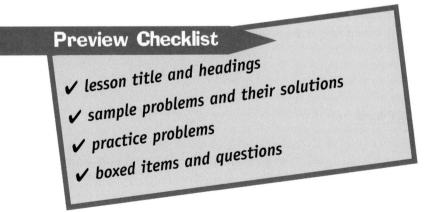

Preview Checklist

✔ lesson title and headings
✔ sample problems and their solutions
✔ practice problems
✔ boxed items and questions

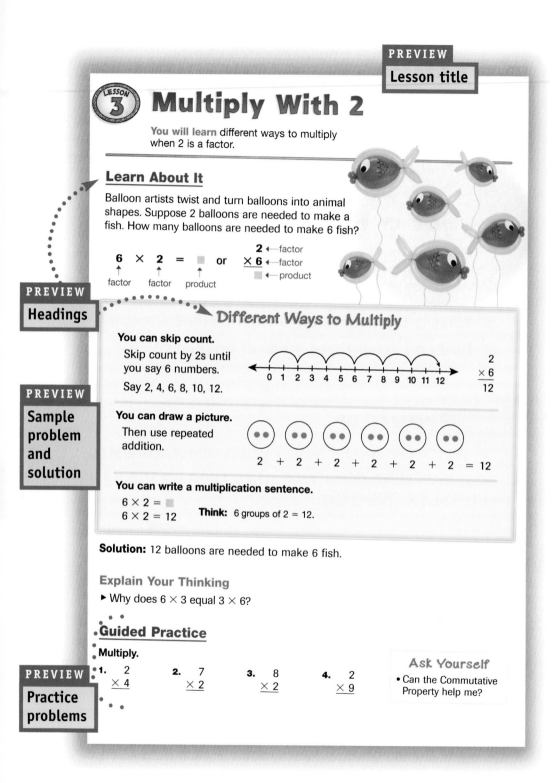

LESSON 3

Multiply With 2

You will learn different ways to multiply when 2 is a factor.

Learn About It

Balloon artists twist and turn balloons into animal shapes. Suppose 2 balloons are needed to make a fish. How many balloons are needed to make 6 fish?

$$6 \times 2 = \blacksquare \quad \text{or} \quad \begin{array}{r} 2 \leftarrow \text{factor} \\ \times 6 \leftarrow \text{factor} \\ \hline \blacksquare \leftarrow \text{product} \end{array}$$

↑ factor   ↑ factor   ↑ product

Different Ways to Multiply

You can skip count.

Skip count by 2s until you say 6 numbers.

Say 2, 4, 6, 8, 10, 12.

$$\begin{array}{r} 2 \\ \times 6 \\ \hline 12 \end{array}$$

You can draw a picture.

Then use repeated addition.

$$2 + 2 + 2 + 2 + 2 + 2 = 12$$

You can write a multiplication sentence.

$6 \times 2 = \blacksquare$
$6 \times 2 = 12$ **Think:** 6 groups of 2 = 12.

Solution: 12 balloons are needed to make 6 fish.

Explain Your Thinking

▶ Why does 6×3 equal 3×6?

Guided Practice

Multiply.

1. $\begin{array}{r} 2 \\ \times 4 \\ \hline \end{array}$ **2.** $\begin{array}{r} 7 \\ \times 2 \\ \hline \end{array}$ **3.** $\begin{array}{r} 8 \\ \times 2 \\ \hline \end{array}$ **4.** $\begin{array}{r} 2 \\ \times 9 \\ \hline \end{array}$

Ask Yourself

• Can the Commutative Property help me?

236

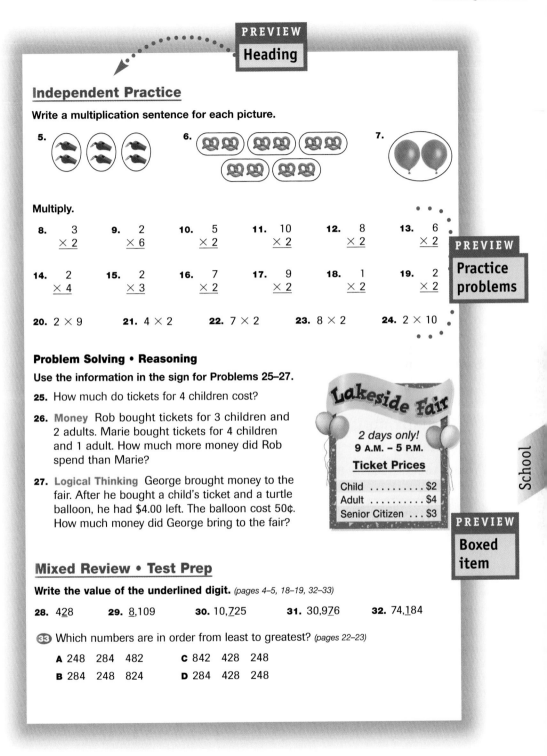

PREVIEW
Heading

Independent Practice

Write a multiplication sentence for each picture.

5.

6.

7.

Multiply.

8.	9.	10.	11.	12.	13.
3 × 2	2 × 6	5 × 2	10 × 2	8 × 2	6 × 2

PREVIEW

Practice problems

14.	15.	16.	17.	18.	19.
2 × 4	2 × 3	7 × 2	9 × 2	1 × 2	2 × 2

20. 2 × 9   **21.** 4 × 2   **22.** 7 × 2   **23.** 8 × 2   **24.** 2 × 10

Problem Solving • Reasoning

Use the information in the sign for Problems 25–27.

25. How much do tickets for 4 children cost?

26. Money Rob bought tickets for 3 children and 2 adults. Marie bought tickets for 4 children and 1 adult. How much more money did Rob spend than Marie?

27. Logical Thinking George brought money to the fair. After he bought a child's ticket and a turtle balloon, he had $4.00 left. The balloon cost 50¢. How much money did George bring to the fair?

Lakeside Fair

2 days only!
9 A.M. – 5 P.M.

Ticket Prices

Child	$2
Adult	$4
Senior Citizen	$3

School

PREVIEW

Boxed item

Mixed Review • Test Prep

Write the value of the underlined digit. *(pages 4–5, 18–19, 32–33)*

28. 4<u>2</u>8   **29.** <u>8</u>,109   **30.** 10,<u>7</u>25   **31.** 30,<u>9</u>76   **32.** 74,1<u>8</u>4

33 Which numbers are in order from least to greatest? *(pages 22–23)*

A 248 284 482   **C** 842 428 248

B 284 248 824   **D** 284 428 248

237

C Plan

What grabbed your attention during your preview? Did you notice any of these ideas?

- ▪ This lesson is about multiplying with 2.
- ▪ There are different ways to multiply.
- ▪ Lots of number and word problems are at the end.

After you finish your preview, you're ready to do your careful reading. First, decide on a strategy. Visualizing and thinking aloud works well with math.

Reading Strategy: Visualizing and Thinking Aloud

Visualizing is a fancy word for making a picture in your mind. When you visualize and think aloud, you "see" something and talk through your ideas about it.

Visualizing

Use the picture from the book to help you understand the problem. Note that each of the six fish is made of two balloons.

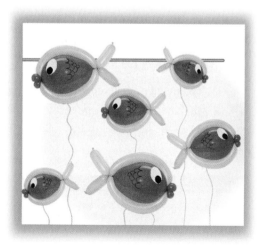

During Reading

Now that you have a plan, you're ready to read the lesson.

D Read with a Purpose

Read slowly and carefully. Remember that every word counts. The first words will tell you the subject of the lesson. But the explanation of how to do the math is usually shown through the examples.

Understand Sample Problems

When you come to a sample problem, try to solve it on your own before you look at the answer. Use the strategy of visualizing and thinking aloud.

Balloon artists twist and turn balloons into animal shapes. Suppose 2 balloons are needed to make a fish. How many balloons are needed to make 6 fish?

$$6 \times 2 = \blacksquare \quad \text{or} \quad \begin{array}{r} 2 \leftarrow \text{factor} \\ \times\, 6 \leftarrow \text{factor} \\ \hline \blacksquare \leftarrow \text{product} \end{array}$$

factor   factor   product

Sample problem

School

Begin by sketching what you "see." Then whisper to yourself the steps you need to take to solve the problem.

Look at this example of how you could use visualizing and thinking aloud to solve the sample problem.

It takes 2 balloons to make 1 fish shape. I want to make 6 fish. First, I'll draw a fish. Then I'll put 2 dots inside to stand for the 2 balloons.

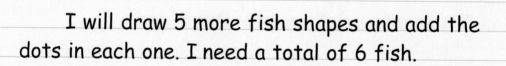

I will draw 5 more fish shapes and add the dots in each one. I need a total of 6 fish.

Then I'll count the number of dots I made. There are 12. This means that 6 x 2 = 12. The answer is 12 balloons. That makes sense. 2 + 2 + 2 + 2 + 2 + 2 = 12.

Solve Practice Problems

Most math lessons have a lot of practice problems.
These give you a chance to use what you've learned.

Multiply.

8.   3
    × 2
	9. 2
	    × 6
		10. 5
		     × 2
			11. 10
			     × 2
				12. 8
				     × 2
					13. 6
					     × 2

14.   2
     × 4
	15. 2
	     × 3
		16. 7
		     × 2
			17. 9
			     × 2
				18. 1
				     × 2
					19. 2
					     × 2

Usually, the easiest practice problems come first. The
problems get harder as you go. If you can't figure out
how to solve a problem, go back to the example. Read
how to do the example problem again.

Try to visualize and think aloud with this next
problem.

This problem asks me to multiply 2 by 4. I'll use a number line. I mark 0 and then add 1, 2, and so on.

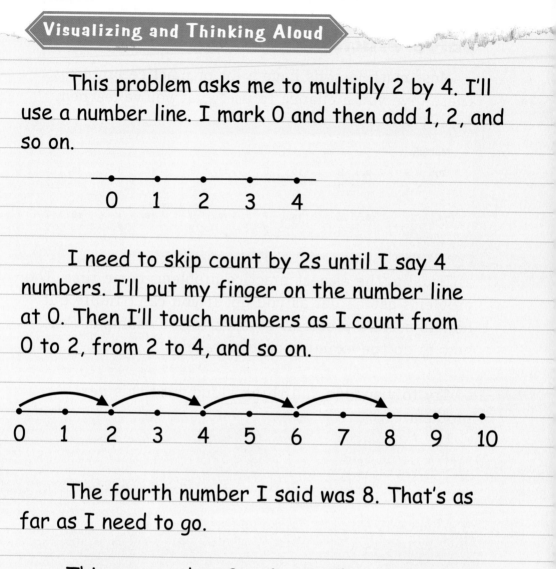

I need to skip count by 2s until I say 4 numbers. I'll put my finger on the number line at 0. Then I'll touch numbers as I count from 0 to 2, from 2 to 4, and so on.

The fourth number I said was 8. That's as far as I need to go.

This means that 2 x 4 = 8. The answer is 8.

Practice on Your Own

Visualizing and thinking aloud can often help you solve math problems. Use sketches and notes when you do a practice problem on your own. Try different ways of solving the problem.

E Connect

One way to make math easier is to think about how you can use it in real life. Ask yourself, "When do I need to multiply with 2?"

Try to connect the lesson to your life.

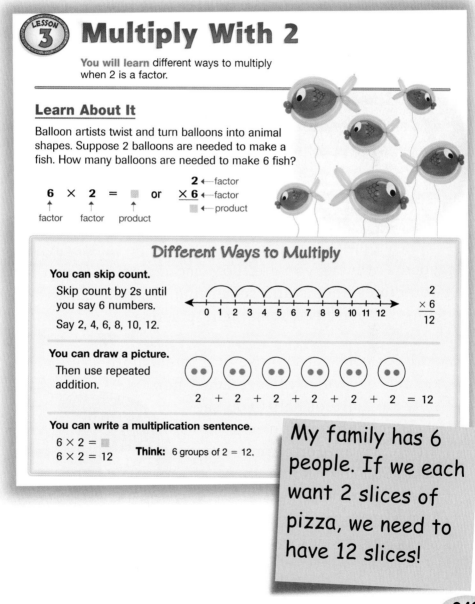

LESSON
3

Multiply With 2

You will learn different ways to multiply when 2 is a factor.

Learn About It

Balloon artists twist and turn balloons into animal shapes. Suppose 2 balloons are needed to make a fish. How many balloons are needed to make 6 fish?

$6 \times 2 = \blacksquare$ or

$$\begin{array}{r} 2 \leftarrow \text{factor} \\ \times 6 \leftarrow \text{factor} \\ \hline \blacksquare \leftarrow \text{product} \end{array}$$

factor factor product

Different Ways to Multiply

You can skip count.

Skip count by 2s until you say 6 numbers.

Say 2, 4, 6, 8, 10, 12.

0 1 2 3 4 5 6 7 8 9 10 11 12

$$\begin{array}{r} 2 \\ \times 6 \\ \hline 12 \end{array}$$

You can draw a picture.

Then use repeated addition.

$2 + 2 + 2 + 2 + 2 + 2 = 12$

You can write a multiplication sentence.

$6 \times 2 = \blacksquare$
$6 \times 2 = 12$

Think: 6 groups of 2 = 12.

School

My family has 6 people. If we each want 2 slices of pizza, we need to have 12 slices!

After Reading

After you finish reading a math lesson, take a deep breath. Then think back on what you've learned.

F Pause and Reflect

When you finish reading a math lesson, it's important to check how well you understood it. Ask yourself some questions.

- **Do I understand how the sample problem was solved?**
- **Can I solve all the practice problems?**
- **Is any part still unclear for me?**

G Reread

Reading math can be a challenge no matter how good a student you are. Do some rereading if you feel you didn't understand something. Or, take time to reread if you need some more practice.

It's a good idea to use a different note-taking tool when you reread. A new note-taking tool helps you see the same information in a different way. For example, try using Summary Notes when you reread. Summary Notes help you think about key ideas.

Summary Notes

MULTIPLYING WITH 2

There are many different ways to multiply with 2.
1. Use a number line.
2. Draw a picture.
3. Write a multiplication sentence.

H Remember

The last step when reading math is to remember what you've learned. If you've read, reread, and practiced the problems, this should be a snap.

But learning math is like learning anything else. You need to *use* what you learned. Try making up a practice problem. Or, have a partner make up a problem too and trade problems. Can you solve these new problems? Solving and talking about them with a partner will help you remember what you've learned.

School

Summing Up

The reading process works well with a math book. Use the strategy of **visualizing and thinking aloud** to help you solve math problems. Summary Notes also work well with math.

Focus on Word Problems

Have you ever read a word problem and thought to yourself, "I'll never figure this out"?

You should know that word problems are often not as hard as they seem. The key to solving them is reading carefully.

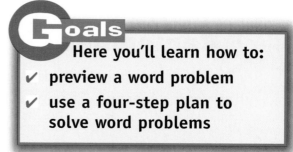

Goals

Here you'll learn how to:

✔ preview a word problem

✔ use a four-step plan to solve word problems

Before Reading

Word problems take time and patience. You may need to read a problem two, three, or even four times. That's okay. Think of your first reading as a quick preview.

Preview a Word Problem

All word problems have two important parts. In one part, you'll find key facts. In the other, you'll find the main question—what you need to find out.

During your preview, look for the main question first. Highlight it. Then look for the key facts. Keep in mind that these might be out of order.

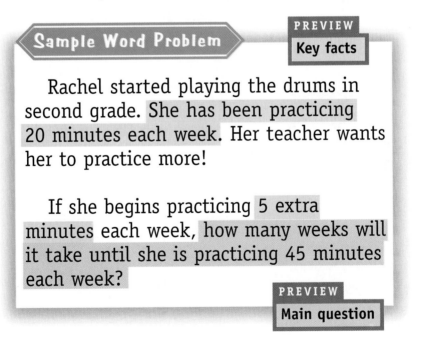

Sample Word Problem

PREVIEW
Key facts

Rachel started playing the drums in second grade. She has been practicing 20 minutes each week. Her teacher wants her to practice more!

If she begins practicing 5 extra minutes each week, how many weeks will it take until she is practicing 45 minutes each week?

PREVIEW
Main question

School

247

Use a Four-step Plan

Having a plan to solve a word problem helps a lot. This plan will work with all types of word problems.

Four-step Plan for Word Problems

Step 1: Read
Read the problem two or three times until it makes sense.

Step 2: Plan
Think of how you can get the answer.

Step 3: Solve
Do the math. Figure out the answer.

Step 4: Check
Check your work. Be sure your answer makes sense.

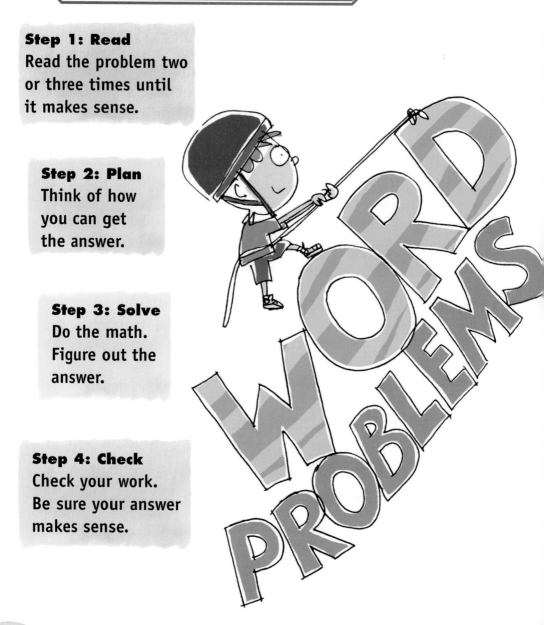

During Reading

Once you finish your preview, it's time to read the problem again and begin solving it.

Step 1: Read

Read (and keep reading) the problem until you understand what it's asking. Cross out any facts or numbers that you don't need.

Start by thinking aloud. Tell yourself what facts you know and what you want to find out.

Think Aloud

I think the main question is "How many weeks will it take until she is practicing 45 minutes each week?"

Here are the key facts.
1. She has been practicing 20 minutes each week up to now.
2. She is going to start practicing 5 more minutes each week.

"More" gives me a clue that I have to use addition to solve the problem.

249

Step 2: Plan

After you understand the main question and know the key facts, decide how you will solve the problem. Try creating a table. Put the minutes Rachel practices on the bottom and the week on the top.

Visualizing

WEEK	1					
MINUTES	20					

Step 3: Solve

After you visualize the information, begin solving the problem. Use the strategy of thinking aloud as you fill in the table you made.

Think Aloud

WEEK	1	2	3	4	5	6
MINUTES	20	25	30	35	40	45

The first week Rachel practiced 20 minutes. I need to add 5 minutes each week until I get to 45. It's week 6 when she practices 45 minutes. The answer is 6 weeks.

Step 4: Check

Always take the time to check your work. Even if the problem was easy for you, you need to be sure that you didn't make a mistake.

To check your answer, try a different way of solving the problem. Once again, you may need to make some notes.

> **Visualizing and Thinking Aloud**

To check my answer, I'll use subtraction. If Rachel practiced for 45 minutes during Week 6, I can subtract 5 to find out how much she practiced during Week 5. That comes to 40. I'll keep subtracting 5 from each week. I get 20 in Week 1.

That's the number Rachel started with! So, my answer of 6 weeks is correct.

45 - Week 6
$\underline{- 5}$
40 - Week 5
$\underline{- 5}$
35 - Week 4
$\underline{- 5}$
30 - Week 3
$\underline{- 5}$
25 - Week 2
$\underline{- 5}$
20 - Week 1

School

After Reading

Sometimes you may have trouble solving a word problem even with the four-step plan. When that happens, don't panic! All it means is that you missed something along the way.

Go back and read the problem again. Be sure you know the main question. List the key facts. Then go through the four steps all over again. If possible, work with a partner.

Summing Up

- **Start by previewing the problem carefully. Highlight the main question and key facts.**
- **Use a four-step plan to solve word problems.**

  Step 1: Read

  Step 2: Plan

  Step 3: Solve

  Step 4: Check

Focus on Questions

Questions, questions, questions. You're surrounded by them! They're in your textbooks. They're on your tests and quizzes. They're on your homework assignments and on the tip of your teacher's tongue.

What should you do with all these questions? Questions can help you learn, but you need to understand a little bit more about them.

In school, you'll see many different types of questions. Some are fact questions. They ask you to answer with specific details from the reading. Others are critical thinking questions. They ask you to draw conclusions using what you know.

Knowing about different kinds of questions can help you answer them.

School

Goals

Here you'll learn how to:

✔ **use a four-step plan to read and answer questions in your textbooks**

✔ **understand the difference between fact and critical thinking questions**

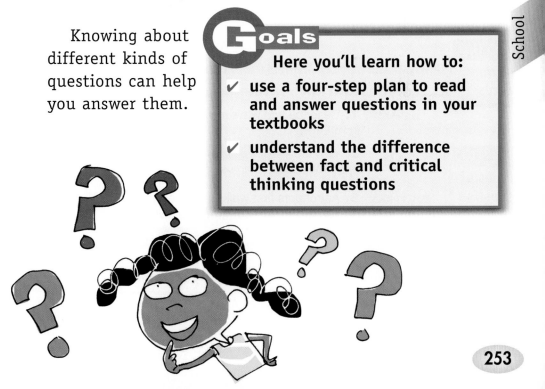

253

Before Reading

Questions can be easy or hard or somewhere in between. The key to answering them is reading carefully. You'll need to read the question itself, and you'll need to read the material the question is based on.

That sounds pretty obvious, right? But you'd be surprised how many students try to answer questions without really reading them.

Preview Questions

Before you read, take a few minutes to preview the questions in a textbook chapter. Notice what types of questions are given. Focus on the key words in each question.

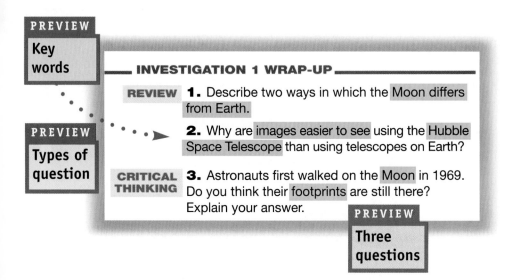

PREVIEW
Key words

PREVIEW
Types of question

INVESTIGATION 1 WRAP-UP

REVIEW **1.** Describe two ways in which the Moon differs from Earth.

2. Why are images easier to see using the Hubble Space Telescope than using telescopes on Earth?

CRITICAL THINKING **3.** Astronauts first walked on the Moon in 1969. Do you think their footprints are still there? Explain your answer.

PREVIEW
Three questions

Use a Four-step Plan

Make it a habit to use this four-step plan for answering questions. You can use it with most types of questions.

Plan for Answering Questions

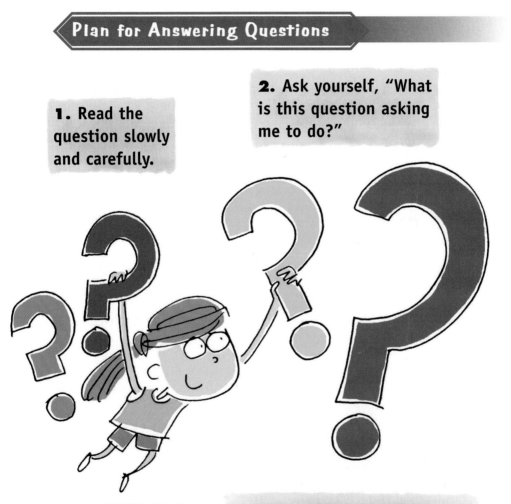

1. Read the question slowly and carefully.

2. Ask yourself, "What is this question asking me to do?"

3. Decide what information you need to answer the question.

4. Find the key words in the question. Then look over the material to find these same key words. Read one sentence before and one sentence after each key word.

School

255

During Reading

Once you've previewed the questions, it's time to use your reading plan.

Answer Fact Questions

Fact questions in a textbook ask you to recall details from your reading. Key words in the question often will match key words in the reading. You can find the answer "right there" in the text. Look at this fact question.

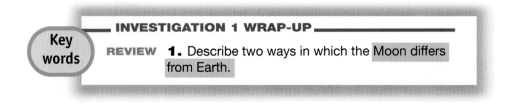

Key words

—— **INVESTIGATION 1 WRAP-UP** ——

REVIEW **1.** Describe two ways in which the Moon differs from Earth.

To answer question 1, skim the textbook chapter. Look at the chapter headings and boldface words. Look for the key words *Moon*, *differs*, and *Earth*.

One difference

Earth is about four times larger than the Moon. That means if the Moon were the size of a tennis ball, Earth would be the size of a basketball.

You need to search in several sentences to find other differences, but the answer is "right there" in the text.

Answer Critical Thinking Questions

The answer to a fact question is somewhere in the text. But, that's not true for a critical thinking question. To answer a critical thinking question, you need to put together information from the text with what you already know.

details from the text + **what I already know** = **my answer**

Read this sample critical thinking question.

> **CRITICAL THINKING** **3.** Astronauts first walked on the Moon in 1969. Do you think their footprints are still there? Explain your answer.
>
> **Key words**

Steps for Critical Thinking Questions

1. Read the question.

2. Decide what the question is asking.
    if footprints from 1969 would still be on the Moon

3. Figure out the information you need.
    what could make footprints disappear

4. Find the key words.
    Moon, footprints

After you read a critical thinking question, stop for a moment. Think about what it's asking. Next, find the parts in the reading that relate to the question. Then read that part carefully.

The Moon has no atmosphere. That's why scientists have found no signs of life there. There is no air to breathe on the Moon. There is no weather. Without air, sound can't travel. So, astronauts on the moon must use two-way radios.

Important details

When you put together what the writer says with what you already know, you can come up with a good answer.

Think Aloud

I think maybe the footprints are still there. But let me think some more. Why <u>wouldn't</u> they still be there?

Sometimes when it rains, water can wash away my footprints. Or, sometimes at the beach, the wind blows hard and covers them up. But the moon has no weather. It doesn't have wind or rain. So I think the footprints are still there.

The answers to some critical thinking questions depend on facts the writer gives and what you already know. The answers to other questions may come almost totally from your own background knowledge.

After Reading

Always take time to check your answers. Reread the question and reread your answer. With each question, ask yourself, "Does my answer make sense? Is there something I should change or add?"

Here are some other questions you can ask yourself when checking your answers:

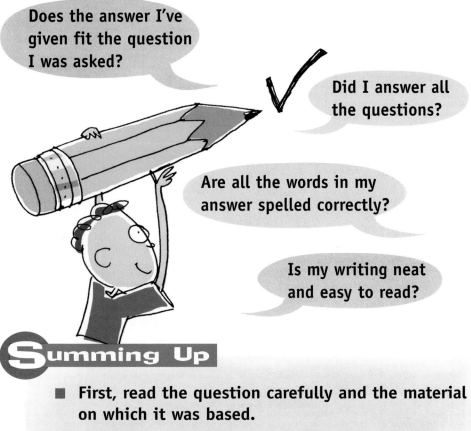

Does the answer I've given fit the question I was asked?

Did I answer all the questions?

Are all the words in my answer spelled correctly?

Is my writing neat and easy to read?

School

Summing Up

- First, read the question carefully and the material on which it was based.
- Look for answers to fact questions right there in the text itself. Search in several sentences.
- For critical thinking questions, put what you've learned with what you already know.

Elements of Textbooks

Every textbook is a little different. But most textbooks have some elements, or parts, in common. It's important that you learn what these elements are and how to use them.

What should you do when you pick up a textbook? First, check to see if there's a table of contents, a glossary, and an index. Look at the headings, graphics, photos, and maps. That should give you a good start.

Elements of Textbooks

Glossary

Most textbooks have a glossary in the back. It tells about the key terms used in the book.

EXAMPLE

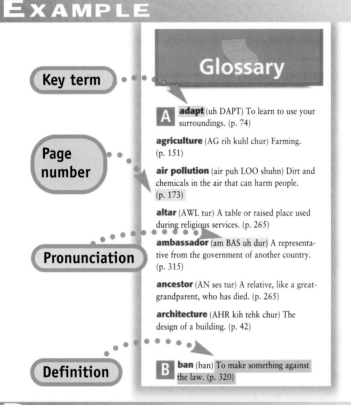

DESCRIPTION

A **glossary** lists in alphabetical order the key terms and their definitions. Sometimes the glossary also provides the pronunciation and page numbers.

Use the glossary to look up key terms as you read. Knowing what these words mean can make it easier for you to understand the textbook.

DEFINITION

A **glossary** is an alphabetical list of a book's key terms and their meanings.

School

Headings and Titles

Think of the headings and titles in a textbook as a way to tell what's to come. You'll find them throughout the text.

EXAMPLE

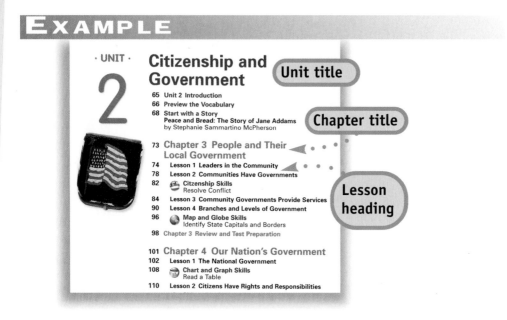

DESCRIPTION

A **heading** describes the content of a section or chapter. The first big heading is usually called the **title.** Read headings and titles on your preview. Get a sense of what you're going to learn about. Use headings to organize your notes and to help you find specific information.

DEFINITION

Headings and titles name the units, chapters, lessons, and smaller parts within the lessons. They are printed in larger type so that they stand out.

Illustrations and Photos

The illustrations and photos in a textbook give information. They help you "see" what is being discussed. They also can give extra information—details that are not covered in the text.

EXAMPLE

The lesser golden plover and the Arctic tern are two kinds of birds that migrate. ▼

Captions

◄ Arctic tern

Photo

Illustration

equator

▲ Lesser golden plover

Caption

School

DESCRIPTION

Illustrations and photos in a textbook make the book more interesting to look at and read. They also give key information. When you look at an illustration or photo, carefully study all of it. Think about how the art fits with the text. Then read the *caption*. It explains the picture and how it connects to the text.

DEFINITION

Illustrations and photos give visual information about a subject.

263

Index

The index appears at the back of a book. It tells on what page to find every important idea, term, person, place, and topic discussed in the book.

EXAMPLE

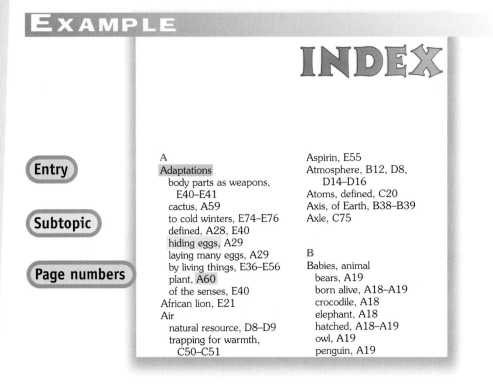

INDEX

Entry

Subtopic

Page numbers

A
Adaptations
  body parts as weapons,
    E40–E41
  cactus, A59
  to cold winters, E74–E76
  defined, A28, E40
  hiding eggs, A29
  laying many eggs, A29
  by living things, E36–E56
  plant, A60
  of the senses, E40
African lion, E21
Air
  natural resource, D8–D9
  trapping for warmth,
    C50–C51

Aspirin, E55
Atmosphere, B12, D8,
    D14–D16
Atoms, defined, C20
Axis, of Earth, B38–B39
Axle, C75

B
Babies, animal
  bears, A19
  born alive, A18–A19
  crocodile, A18
  elephant, A18
  hatched, A18–A19
  owl, A19
  penguin, A19

DESCRIPTION

Use the **index** to help you find specific information in a textbook. Some main topics are broken down into smaller subtopics. Each entry includes the page numbers where you'll find information about that topic.

DEFINITION

An **index** lists ideas, terms, people, places, and topics in a textbook to help you find them.

Maps

Maps provide information. They show the exact location of the countries, cities, and states discussed in the textbook. They can also show land features such as mountains and rivers.

EXAMPLE

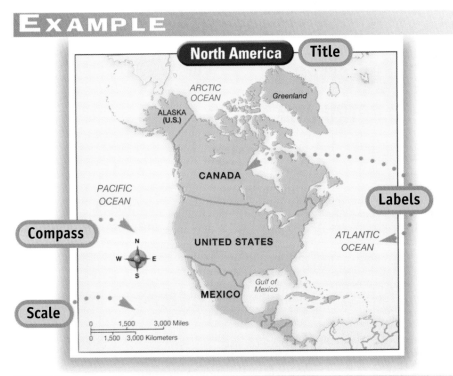

DESCRIPTION

Every **map** has a few main parts. The *title* tells you what the map is about. The *scale* lets you measure distance. The *compass* tells which direction is north, south, east, and west. Some maps have a *key* that tells you what the map's symbols and colors mean.

DEFINITION

Maps are like information pictures. They can show a location and what it's like.

School

Previews

Many textbook units or chapters open with a preview or study box. Its purpose is to introduce major topics, key vocabulary, and important ideas about the subject.

EXAMPLE

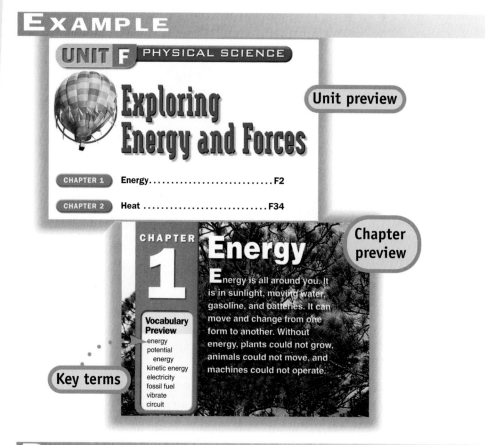

DESCRIPTION

Think of **previews** as warm-ups to the subject you're going to be reading about. They get you ready to read. Previews can include photographs, questions, vocabulary lists, outlines, or even photos.

DEFINITION

A **preview** is the opening part of a book or chapter. It prepares you for what you're about to read.

Table of Contents

The table of contents in a book lists the major parts.
It tells the page on which every major part begins.

EXAMPLE

DESCRIPTION

The **table of contents** is an outline, or overview, of a book. It lists all the units, chapters, and lesson titles. Use the table of contents as you would a road map. It can help you find your way through a text.

DEFINITION

The **table of contents** lists the major parts of a book and their page numbers. The table of contents can help you find specific parts of a book quickly and easily.

School

Reading
Stories and Poems

Reading Kinds of Literature

Reading a Folktale
Reading a Novel
Reading a Poem

Focus on Stories

Focus on Plot
Focus on Characters
Focus on Setting

Elements of Literature

Reading a Folktale

Remember the story of Little Red Riding Hood? That kind of story is called a folktale.

Folktales are made-up stories—stories that did not really happen. They are one of the oldest kinds of stories in the world. People all around the world tell them, usually to teach children an important lesson about life. Do you know any folktales?

Goals

Here you'll learn how to:

✔ **read and understand folktales**

✔ **use the reading strategy of summarizing**

Before Reading

Before you read a folktale, take a few minutes to get ready. Set a purpose, preview, and make a plan for reading.

FREE YOURSELF FROM TRAPS

A Set a Purpose

Most of the time you will probably read a folktale just for fun.

But what should you look for as you read? These two questions will help you set your purpose.

■ **What happens in the folktale?**

■ **What is the main lesson to be learned?**

B Preview

Take a few minutes to preview the folktale "The Lion and the Mouse." If you preview a story before you read, you'll understand it better. Look for these items as you preview:

Preview Checklist

✔ *title*

✔ *repeated words or phrases*

✔ *first and last paragraphs*

✔ *pictures or photos*

Look quickly over each page. Don't try to read every word in every sentence. You can do that later.

Stories and Poems

271

PREVIEW
Title

The Lion and the Mouse
by Jerry Pinkney

PREVIEW
First
paragraph

One day while a mouse was creeping through the tall grass, she happened upon a great lion asleep in the sun. "I might see for quite a long distance from the top of that beast's back," she thought. Boldly the mouse crept up the lion's flank and scampered along his spine.

The tickling of the mouse's tiny feet woke the lion. With one swipe he snatched her in his claws and dangled her by her tail in front of his nose. "For daring to interrupt my nap," the lion growled, "you'll be my next meal!"

PREVIEW
Repeated
words

"Oh, please," the terrified mouse gasped, "let me go, and I promise one day I'll help you in return."

The lion shook with laughter. "Impossible!" he roared. But the proud animal was so amused by the idea that he allowed the mouse to go.

Not long after, the lion was caught in a trap set by some clever hunters. No matter how the powerful beast thrashed and fought, he could not free himself from the strong net that raised him from the ground. No other animal dared come near to help

"The Lion and the Mouse," continued

for fear of the hunters. But when the brave little mouse heard his cries, she remembered her promise and hurried to his side. Quickly she gnawed through the sturdy ropes with her sharp teeth until the lion could escape to freedom.

"You see," she said, "there are times when even a tiny mouse can help a lion."

Even the strongest can sometimes use the help of the smallest.

PREVIEW
Last paragraph

PREVIEW
Picture

Plan

You probably learned facts like these during your preview of "The Lion and the Mouse."

- The characters are a mouse and a lion.
- The setting is in the tall grass.
- The mouse crawls up the lion's back.
- Something happens to the lion, and the mouse helps.
- The folktale ends with a lesson.

When you finish previewing, it's time to make a plan for reading. Remember your purposes for reading.

What happens in the folktale?

What is the main lesson to be learned?

What strategy can help you learn what you want? One good strategy for folktales is summarizing.

Reading Strategy: **Summarizing**

Summarizing means telling the main events and ideas in your own words. A summary is much shorter than the whole story. That's because you leave out many details. You only tell the most important events.

A Story String is a good reading tool to use with a folktale. A Story String can help you remember important events and keep them in the right order. Make a box for only the most important parts of the story.

Story String

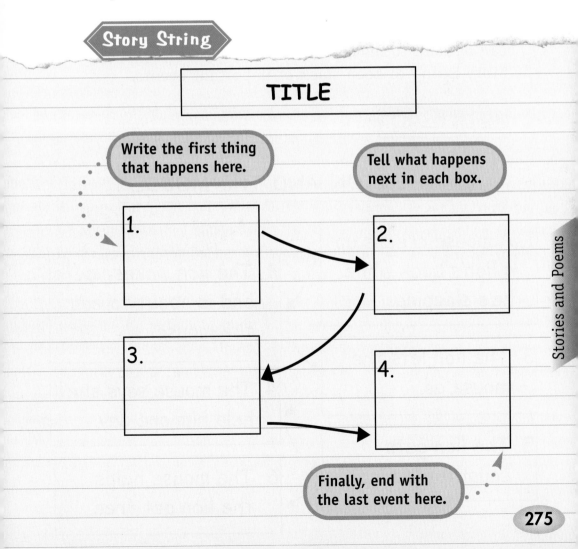

TITLE

Write the first thing that happens here.

Tell what happens next in each box.

1.

2.

3.

4.

Finally, end with the last event here.

Stories and Poems

275

During Reading

Now you are ready to read "The Lion and the Mouse."

D Read with a Purpose

Remember, your purpose is to find out what happens in the folktale and what the main lesson is. As you read, you may want to take notes.

Keep Track of Events

On each page, lots of things happen. That's why it can be hard to remember all of the details. Fill in your Story String to keep track of important events.

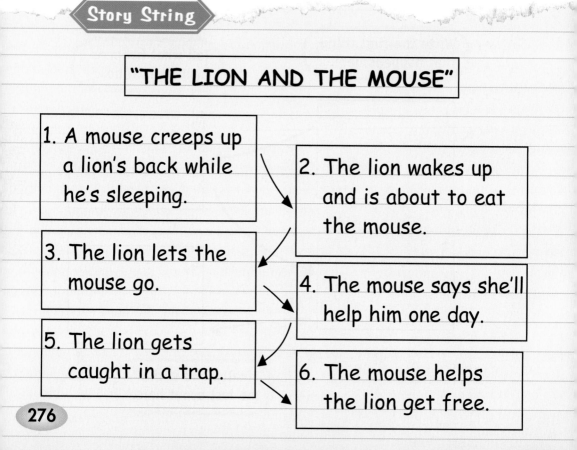

Story String

"THE LION AND THE MOUSE"

1. A mouse creeps up a lion's back while he's sleeping.

2. The lion wakes up and is about to eat the mouse.

3. The lion lets the mouse go.

4. The mouse says she'll help him one day.

5. The lion gets caught in a trap.

6. The mouse helps the lion get free.

Look for Important Characters

Pay attention to the main characters as you read a folktale. It's fun to see what characters say and do. Decide what you think of them. What do you notice about the lion and the mouse in this part of the story? Look for words that tell you about the characters.

from "The Lion and the Mouse"

"Oh, please," the terrified mouse gasped, "let me go, and I promise one day I'll help you in return."

The lion shook with laughter. "Impossible!" he roared. But the proud animal was so amused by the idea that he allowed the mouse to go.

> The mouse is scared but smart.

> The lion thinks he is so great and strong.

You can easily tell who the two main characters are in this folktale. But the more you can find out about what the lion and the mouse are really like, the better you'll understand what you're reading.

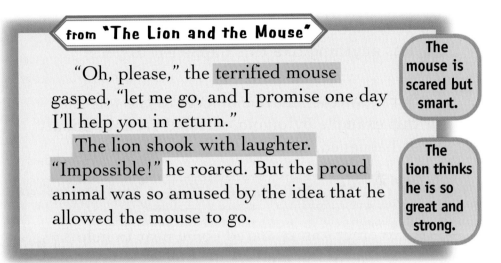

Stories and Poems

E Connect

As you read, try to connect your life to the story. Here are some questions to get you started.

- How would you feel if you were the lion?
- Do you think the mouse did the right thing?
- What do you think of the lesson of the folktale?
- Has anything like this happened to you?

Note how the reader connects to the folktale in this example by giving personal feelings about what happened.

from "The Lion and the Mouse"

No other animal dared come near to help for fear of the hunters. But when the brave little mouse heard his cries, she remembered her promise and hurried to his side. Quickly she gnawed through the sturdy ropes with her sharp teeth until the lion could escape to freedom.

"You see," she said, "there are times when even a tiny mouse can help a lion."

Even the strongest can sometimes use the help of the smallest.

I'm glad she kept her promise.

I think this is true. When I was little, I helped my dad find his keys.

After Reading

When you finish reading a folktale, think for a minute about what you learned. Reflecting on what you read will help you understand and remember the story better.

F Pause and Reflect

Think again about your reading purpose. Can you answer these questions now?

> Do I know what the main lesson is?

> Do I know what happens in the folktale?

> Is there anything that confuses me?

> Can I describe what the main characters are like?

You may have forgotten some of the details. Maybe you can't remember how the story started. Or maybe you're not sure why a character did or said something. One way to fix up your understanding is to reread parts of the folktale.

Stories and Poems

G Reread

Most of the time you won't need to reread the whole folktale. Instead, you'll want to look at just a couple of parts. Skim back over the pages. Find the parts you had trouble understanding or remembering. Go back and reread them.

For example, let's say you're not sure why the mouse ever went near the lion in the first place. Go back to the first paragraph.

from "The Lion and the Mouse"

One day while a mouse was creeping through the tall grass, she happened upon a great lion asleep in the sun. "I might see for quite a long distance from the top of that beast's back," she thought. Boldly the mouse crept up the lion's flank and scampered along his spine.

> **What the mouse is thinking**

By rereading, you learn that the mouse climbed on the lion to get a good view.

H Remember

The best way to remember what you read is to talk or write about it. Tell a friend what you like about the folktale or take notes in an organizer.

Here's a way to use a Fiction Organizer to pull together the most important parts of a story.

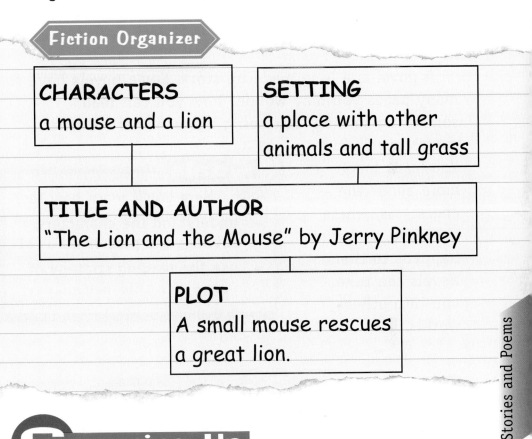

Fiction Organizer

CHARACTERS
a mouse and a lion

SETTING
a place with other animals and tall grass

TITLE AND AUTHOR
"The Lion and the Mouse" by Jerry Pinkney

PLOT
A small mouse rescues a great lion.

Stories and Poems

Summing Up

When you read a folktale, try using the strategy of **summarizing.** Two reading tools can help you understand and remember a folktale:

■ Story String   ■ Fiction Organizer

Reading a Novel

Maybe you're just beginning to read your first or second novel on your own. Or maybe you've already read many novels. Knowing how to use reading strategies and tools can help you read novels even better.

A novel is a long made-up story. Some novels have so many pages you may wonder how you can read something so long. But being longer is part of what makes novels fun. You learn much more about the characters, where they live, and what happens to them. Novels can take you into other worlds.

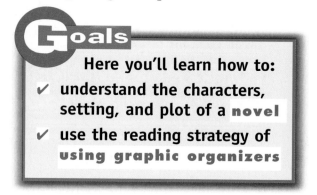

Goals

Here you'll learn how to:
- ✔ understand the characters, setting, and plot of a **novel**
- ✔ use the reading strategy of **using graphic organizers**

Before Reading

Before reading a novel, you should set a purpose, preview, and make a plan for reading.

A Set a Purpose

Ask yourself, "Why am I reading this novel?" Are you reading just for fun or for a school assignment? Either way, here are three questions that you'll want to be able to answer.

■ **What happens in the novel?**
■ **Who are the main characters in the novel?**
■ **Where and when does the action take place?**

B Preview

You may find novels hard to preview. Their titles and chapter names may or may not tell you what the novel is about. To preview a novel well, you need to know *where* to look. Look for these items:

Preview Checklist

✔ title and author
✔ front and back covers
✔ table of contents or chapter titles
✔ pictures
✔ first couple of paragraphs

Stories and Poems

Front Cover

PREVIEW
Picture

PREVIEW
Title

PREVIEW
Author

A Trophy Chapter Book

FLAT STANLEY

He leads a very *full* life!

By Jeff Brown
Illustrated by Steve Björkman

Back Cover

A Trophy Chapter Book

Four feet tall.
One foot wide.
Half an inch thick.

PREVIEW
Main character

PREVIEW
Plot

Stanley Lambchop is a nice, average boy. He leads a nice, ordinary life. Then one day a bulletin board falls on him and suddenly Stanley is flat.

This turns out to be very interesting. Stanley gets rolled up, mailed, and flown like a kite. He even gets to stop crime. He's flat, but he's a hero!

Join him for a series of very funny, very unusual adventures:
Flat Stanley
Stanley and the Magic Lamp
Invisible Stanley

US $4.25 / $6.25 CAN
ISBN 0-06-442026-4

HarperTrophy®
0710

Cover art © 1996 by Steve Björkman

The front and back covers tell you what to expect in *Flat Stanley*. Now preview the table of contents and the first couple of paragraphs of the novel.

Table of Contents

CONTENTS

PREVIEW
Chapter titles

Beginning of Novel

PREVIEW
First paragraphs

PREVIEW
Character names

Breakfast was ready.

"I will go wake the boys," Mrs. Lambchop said to her husband, George Lambchop. Just then their younger son, Arthur, called from the bedroom he shared with his brother, Stanley.

"Hey! Come and look! Hey!"

Mr. and Mrs. Lambchop were both very much in favor of politeness and careful speech. "Hay is for horses, Arthur, not people," Mr. Lambchop said as they entered the bedroom. "Try to remember that."

Stories and Poems

C Plan

Think about what you found out about *Flat Stanley* from your preview. You already know a lot of information.

- Stanley Lambchop is a boy who becomes flat.
- Lots of interesting things happen to Stanley.
- Stanley lives with his parents and brother.
- The novel is going to be funny.

Reading Strategy: Using Graphic Organizers

Graphic organizers are "word pictures." They can be charts, lists, or pictures. Using graphic organizers helps you see what's important in a novel and how all the parts fit together.

A Fiction Organizer is a good tool to help you find and remember the important details of a novel.

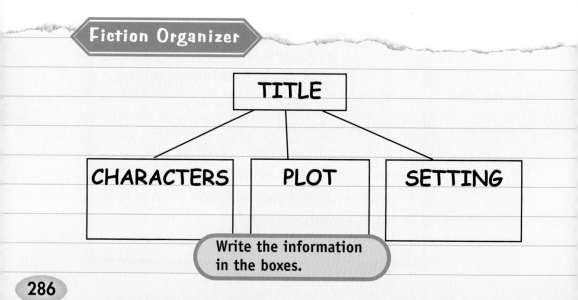

Fiction Organizer

TITLE

CHARACTERS   PLOT   SETTING

Write the information in the boxes.

During Reading

You have set a purpose, previewed, and made a plan. You're warmed up and ready. Now it's time to read more of *Flat Stanley*.

D Read with a Purpose

As you read, you'll want to learn about the plot, the characters, and the setting.

1. Plot

The *plot* is the action of the novel. Plot is what happens. The events may be exciting, scary, silly, or sad. The plot of a story can be about almost anything— from tornadoes and baseball games to magical coins.

In many stories, the plot is about a character that has a problem to solve. Here you learn about Stanley's problem right away. A bulletin board has fallen on him while he was sleeping.

> **from *Flat Stanley* by Jeff Brown**
>
> "Heavens!" said Mrs. Lambchop.   Stanley's problem
> "Gosh!" said Arthur. "Stanley's flat!"
> "As a pancake," said Mr. Lambchop.
> "Darndest thing I've ever seen."

The plot of the book is about what happens to Stanley when he's flat.

Stories and Poems

287

2. Characters

The *characters* are the people, animals, or things that take part in the action. Watch what they say and do, how they feel, and what others think of them.

from *Flat Stanley*

When Stanley got used to being flat, he enjoyed it. He could go in and out of rooms, even when the door was closed, just by lying down and sliding through the crack at the bottom.

> Stanley likes being flat.

Use a Character Map to take notes on what a character is like. Here's an example of a Character Map.

Character Map

WHAT HE SAYS AND DOES He goes under doors.	**WHAT OTHERS THINK** His parents are amazed.
STANLEY	
HOW HE LOOKS AND FEELS He likes being flat.	**HOW I FEEL** I'm surprised that he is not upset.

3. Setting

The *setting* is where and when the novel takes place. In some novels, everything happens in just one place and time. In other novels, characters move around from place to place. Days, weeks, or even years go by.

Sometimes the setting is very important. It affects the mood, what the characters do, and how they feel. In other novels, such as *Flat Stanley*, the setting is less important. The silly things that happen to him after he's flat could happen almost anywhere.

Try to picture the setting in your mind as you read. Ask yourself, "Where is this?" "When is this happening?" For example, where is Stanley here?

from *Flat Stanley*

Arthur let out all the string, and Stanley soared high above the trees, a beautiful sight in his red and blue trousers, against the pale-blue sky.
Everyone in the park stood still to watch.

Where Stanley is

Setting is the park.

Stories and Poems

Sometimes you will want to collect your notes about plot, characters, and setting in one place. On the next page, you'll find an example of an organizer you could use.

CHARACTERS
Stanley, Mrs. Lambchop, Mr. Lambchop, Arthur

SETTING
a city with big buildings and a park

TITLE
Flat Stanley

PLOT
Stanley gets flattened by a bulletin board. But he still has a lot of fun and adventures. At the end, he goes back to his normal shape.

A Fiction Organizer helps you keep track of all the key information in a novel. You can add to the organizer as you read. Or, you can wait until you're done reading to fill it out. This organizer contains everything you would need to get started on a book report about *Flat Stanley*.

E Connect

You'll like what you read and remember it better if you can connect to it. Ask yourself questions like these to connect your life to a novel.

■ How do I feel about the characters?

■ How do I feel about what happens to them?

■ What in the novel reminds me of my own life?

■ What else have I read like this before?

Here is an example of how one reader connected to *Flat Stanley*.

from *Flat Stanley*

Stanley told his parents how he felt. "It's the other kids I mostly mind," he said. "They don't like me anymore because I'm different. Flat."

"Shame on them," Mrs. Lambchop said. "It is wrong to dislike people for their shapes. Or their religion, for that matter, or the color of their skin."

She's right! I agree.

How do *you* feel about what Mrs. Lambchop says?

Stories and Poems

After Reading

After you finish reading a novel, you might feel like just putting the book away. But it's a good idea to stop and think a little about the novel you just finished.

F Pause and Reflect

Think for a minute about the questions you had *before* you began reading. Can you answer all of them?

What happens in the novel?

Where and when does the action take place?

Who are the main characters in the novel?

G Reread

Novels are full of many details. You can easily forget something or be confused about a certain part. Or, maybe you have a favorite scene that makes you laugh. Go back and reread parts that you really like.

H Remember

After you finish a novel, do something to help you remember it. Talk about the book with a friend or create a Storyboard.

A Storyboard helps you remember what happened.

Storyboard

FLAT STANLEY

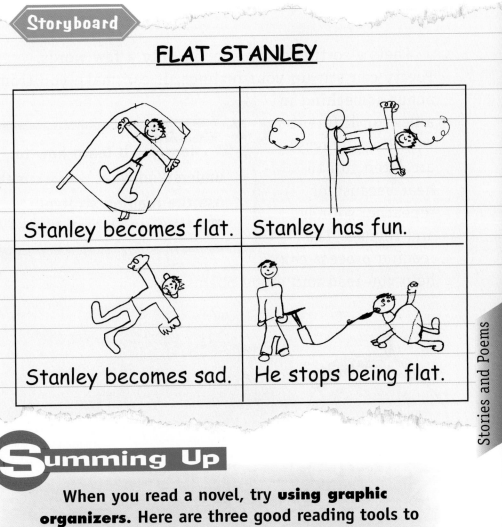

Stanley becomes flat.	Stanley has fun.
Stanley becomes sad.	He stops being flat.

Stories and Poems

Summing Up

When you read a novel, try **using graphic organizers.** Here are three good reading tools to help you understand a novel:

- Fiction Organizer
- Character Map
- Storyboard

Reading a Poem

A poem looks different from a story or an article. Poems are often written in short lines and have interesting shapes, rhymes, or sounds. Do you have a favorite poem?

Poets also try to say a lot in only a few words. Poetry can stir up your feelings. It can make you think about something in a new or different way. Many poems are often fun to hear because of repeating sounds and rhymes. The reading process can help you read and enjoy poems.

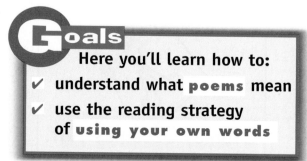

Goals

Here you'll learn how to:

✔ understand what **poems** mean
✔ use the reading strategy of **using your own words**

Before Reading

Before you read a poem, first set a purpose. Next, preview the poem and choose a plan for reading.

A Set a Purpose

Maybe you are reading a poem for fun or for a school assignment. Either way, you'll want to answer two questions.

- **What is this poem saying?**
- **What makes this poem special?**

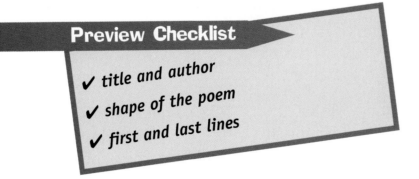

B Preview

Now preview "Michael Is Afraid of the Storm" on the next page. Look for the items on this checklist. Touch each item with your finger when you find it.

Preview Checklist

✔ title and author
✔ shape of the poem
✔ first and last lines

Stories and Poems

295

PREVIEW

Title and author

"Michael Is Afraid of the Storm"
by Gwendolyn Brooks

PREVIEW

First line

1 Lightning is angry in the night.
Thunder spanks our house.
Rain is hating our old elm —
It punishes the boughs.

PREVIEW

Three groups of lines

2 Now, I am next to nine years old,
And crying's not for me.
But if I touch my mother's hand,
Perhaps no one will see.

PREVIEW

Last line

3 And if I keep herself in sight —
Follow her busy dress —
No one will notice my wild eye.
No one will laugh, I guess.

Plan

Your preview of this poem tells you many things.

■ The poem is about a boy named Michael.

■ There's a big storm, and Michael is afraid.

■ The poem has three parts.

You've learned a lot. Now read the poem slowly. You can learn a lot more from the poem by reading it carefully two or three times. But what strategy should you use?

Reading Strategy: Using Your Own Words

Sometimes a poem can be hard to figure out. To check your understanding, try putting things in your own words. Read a line or two. Think about what they mean. Then use your own words to say the same thing.

A Double-entry Journal works well to help you put something you read into your own words. Write down key words, phrases, or lines from the poem in the first column. Then, write down what you think they mean in the other column.

Double-entry Journal

QUOTES	MY WORDS

Write lines of the poem here.

Use your own words to write what they mean here.

Stories and Poems

During Reading

Now you are ready to read "Michael Is Afraid of the Storm." Go slowly, and read it with care.

D Read with a Purpose

As you read, remember your purpose. You want to understand what the poem is saying and what makes it special. Plan on reading the poem three times.

1. First Reading—Meaning

When you first read the poem, you begin to figure out what it means. Write down a few words or phrases that seem important. Then put those thoughts into your own words.

Double-entry Journal

QUOTES	MY WORDS
"Lightning is angry in the night."	Lightning _is_ so scary. It's like someone gets mad all of a sudden.
"And crying's not for me."	Kids my age should not cry.

In a poem, every single word may be important. If you aren't sure what a word means, you may need to look it up.

from "Michael Is Afraid of the Storm"

Lightning is angry in the night.
Thunder spanks our house.
Rain is hating our old elm—
It punishes the boughs.

New word

Let's say you are reading the poem and stop on one word in the last line of the first *stanza,* or group of lines. You've never seen the word *boughs* before and don't know what it means. You're not even sure how to pronounce it. If there's no one to ask, look it up in a dictionary. The **s** on the end means it's probably a plural word—more than one. So when you look in the dictionary, look for *bough.*

bough – a main branch of a tree

Now the last two lines make sense. Rain is falling on an elm tree. The storm is beating down on the tree branches. The whole first part of the poem tells how strong the storm is.

Stories and Poems

2. Second Reading—Sound and Shape

Now read the poem again. This time pay attention to the sounds in the poem and how the poem is organized.

SOUND

What do you think of how this poem sounds? Look for rhymes and repeated words and sounds.

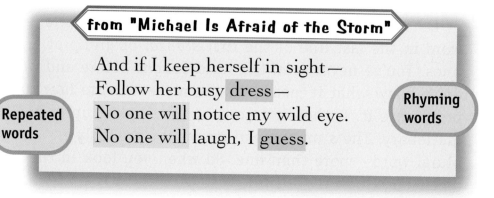

from "Michael Is Afraid of the Storm"

And if I keep herself in sight—
Follow her busy dress—
No one will notice my wild eye.
No one will laugh, I guess.

Repeated words

Rhyming words

Did you notice any rhymes? Look at the second and fourth lines. The words *dress* and *guess* rhyme. The rhymes and repeated words help make this poem sound interesting.

SHAPE

What is the shape of this poem? How is it organized? Did you see it has three separate parts? Each part is called a *stanza*.

Each stanza in a poem contains a different idea, like a paragraph in a story. The first stanza describes the storm. The second stanza gives details about Michael. The third stanza tells about Michael's plan to stay near his mother.

3. Third Reading—Language

Poets have special ways of using language. Sometimes poets compare one thing to something else so that you'll think about things in a new and different way. Here are three common kinds of comparisons poets use.

SIMILE

A *simile* is a comparison of two things using the words *like* or *as*. An example is "Lightning is like an angry person."

METAPHOR

A *metaphor* is also a comparison of two things, but without the words *like* or *as*. An example of a metaphor is "Lightning is an angry person."

PERSONIFICATION

Personification is also common in poetry. You find this when a poet makes an animal, object, or idea seem human. Can you find personification in "Michael Is Afraid of the Storm"? Read the first stanza again.

from "Michael Is Afraid of the Storm"

Lightning is angry in the night.
Thunder spanks our house.
Rain is hating our old elm—
It punishes the boughs.

The storm
seems human.

Stories and Poems

The storm does things a person would do. It gets angry. It spanks the house and punishes the tree. That's an example of personification.

E Connect

When you read a poem, make connections to your own life.

■ What does the poem remind you of in your life?
■ How do you feel as you read the poem?
■ What do you think of it?

Here's how one reader connected to this poem.

"Michael Is Afraid of the Storm"

Lightning is angry in the night.
Thunder spanks our house.
Rain is hating our old elm—
It punishes the boughs.

Now, I am next to nine years old,
And crying's not for me.
But if I touch my mother's hand,
Perhaps no one will see.

And if I keep herself in sight—
Follow her busy dress—
No one will notice my wild eye.
No one will laugh, I guess.

I never thought of a storm this way. I like these lines.

I used to cry when I heard thunder.

After Reading

After you finish reading a poem, stop and think about it for a while.

F Pause and Reflect

Remember your purpose for reading the poem. Do you know the answers to these questions?

- **What is this poem saying?**
- **What makes this poem special?**
- **Can I explain the poem in my own words?**

Maybe you aren't sure about the answers to these questions. That's okay. You can always go back and reread.

G Reread

Sometimes you may decide to reread just a couple of lines of a poem. Other times you will want to read the whole poem again. How much you reread depends on how much time you have and what questions you still have about the poem.

For example, let's say you didn't really understand the end of the poem. Reread the last stanza. Think about what it means.

Stories and Poems

And if I keep herself in sight—
Follow her busy dress—
No one will notice my wild eye.
No one will laugh, I guess.

Words to
think about

Think Aloud

At first, I didn't get the part about the "busy dress." But now I think the "busy dress" is just a way of saying that the mother is moving around a lot.

I think Michael's eye is "wild" because he is scared. Maybe he's about to cry.

Talking through your ideas about a poem in a Think Aloud can help you understand it better.

H Remember

What can you do to remember a poem you've read? It's easier to remember a poem when you talk or write about it. Here are some things to try.

■ Share the poem with a friend.

■ Read it out loud.

■ Copy your favorite line or two in your Reading Notebook.

■ Say what the poem means in one sentence of your own.

Summing Up

When you read a poem, use the reading process and strategy of **using your own words.** Try to read the poem three times. Two reading tools can help you understand and remember the poem:

■ **Double-entry Journal**

■ **Think Aloud**

Stories and Poems

Focus on Plot

What happens in a story is called the plot. It's the action. The plot is made up of the events that happen from the beginning to the end of the story.

Sometimes plots tell about things that seem like they could happen to you. For example, a plot might be about going to school, taking a trip, or meeting a new person. Other times plots are about more unusual things, such as talking animals, magical places, or times long ago.

Good plots keep you interested in the story. You turn the page because you want to find out what happens next. Use the reading process to help you understand a story's plot.

Goals

Here you'll learn how to:

✔ **keep track of the events of a plot**

✔ **understand how the parts of a plot work together**

Before Reading

When you begin a story, you want to know right away who's in it, what's going on, and where the story is taking place.

Background Information

A story usually starts by giving you background information. You can often find out a lot in the first one or two paragraphs.

Try previewing the first part of *The Skirt*.

PREVIEW

Main character

from *The Skirt* by Gary Soto

After stepping off the bus, Miata Ramirez turned around and gasped, "Ay!" The school bus lurched, coughed a puff of stinky exhaust, and made a wide turn at the corner. The driver strained as he worked the steering wheel like the horns of a bull. Miata yelled for the driver to stop. She started running after the bus. Her hair whipped against her shoulders. A large book bag tugged at her arm with each running step, and bead earrings jingled as they banged against her neck.

PREVIEW

What she's doing

Stories and Poems

Miata just got off a bus and starts running after it. Why do you think she wants the bus to stop?

The Problem

From your preview, you know where the main character is and what she is doing. But what happens next? You are just beginning to learn Miata's problem.

from _The Skirt_

Miata's problem

"My skirt!" she cried loudly. "Stop!"
She had forgotten her *folklórico* skirt. It was still on the bus.

She needed that skirt. On Sunday after church she was going to dance *folklórico*. Her troupe had practiced for three months. If she was the only girl without a costume, her parents would wear sunglasses out of embarrassment. Miata didn't want that.

Why she is upset

The main problem in this story is that Miata left her skirt on the school bus. The title of the book makes more sense now, doesn't it?

During Reading

As you read, you'll want to keep track of specific events in the plot. One easy way to do that is to note what happens in the beginning, the middle, and the end.

The Beginning

The beginning of a story puts you in a specific place and time. You meet the characters and find out about a problem they have.

Take your time, especially in the beginning. It can give you lots of important information.

from *The Skirt*

The skirt had belonged to her mother when she was a child in Hermosillo, Mexico. What is Mom going to think? Miata asked herself. Her mother was always scolding Miata for losing things.

The skirt is special.

Miata's mother had the skirt when she was a child in Mexico. That's why leaving it on the bus is such a big problem. It's a special skirt.

Stories and Poems

The Middle

In the middle part of a story, the characters face the problem and try to solve it. In most stories, the problem isn't solved right away. What the characters try first often doesn't work.

Most plots have a *climax*, or turning point. That's where the problem is about to be solved. The problem is at its worst at the climax. At that point, you're the most caught up in the story and interested in what's happening.

Here is the climax of *The Skirt*. Miata and her friend Ana see the skirt in a bus in the school parking lot. Ana tries to open the door and get in without anyone seeing them.

from *The Skirt*

"You can do it," Miata encouraged again.

Ana reached until her arm hurt from stretching. When her hand clasped the lever, she pulled and yanked. And Miata pulled and yanked on Ana.

The lever gave, and the door opened with a sigh.

"*¡Qué bueno!*" Miata cheered, hugging her friend. They smiled widely at each other.

> They get the bus door open.

The End

In the end, things usually work out for the characters. The ending of most stories tells you how the problem is solved. In *The Skirt*, the ending is a happy one.

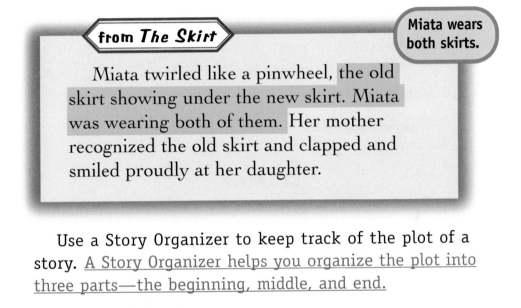

from *The Skirt*

Miata wears both skirts.

Miata twirled like a pinwheel, the old skirt showing under the new skirt. Miata was wearing both of them. Her mother recognized the old skirt and clapped and smiled proudly at her daughter.

Use a Story Organizer to keep track of the plot of a story. A Story Organizer helps you organize the plot into three parts—the beginning, middle, and end.

Story Organizer

TITLE The Skirt		
BEGINNING	**MIDDLE**	**END**
Miata forgets her skirt on the school bus.	Miata and her friend try to get the skirt.	Miata gets the skirt but gets a new one too.

Stories and Poems

After Reading

After you finish reading a story or novel, try to tell what happened to a friend. Reread parts of the story if you can't remember the plot.

You might also want to make a Plot Diagram of a story. A Plot Diagram shows how specific parts of a plot fit together. Here is a sample Plot Diagram for *The Skirt*.

Plot Diagram

CLIMAX
Miata and her friend sneak onto a bus to get it.

PROBLEM
Miata has to get her skirt back.

SOLUTION
She wears two skirts to the dance.

Summing Up

- Think about how the events in the beginning, middle, and end fit together.
- Look for the problem that a character faces, the climax, and the solution.
- Use a Story Organizer or a Plot Diagram to help you keep track of plot details.

Focus on Characters

Close your eyes and think of a story you really like. What makes it one of your favorites? One thing you probably like is the characters—the people, animals, or creatures that the story is about.

Characters are important in stories and novels. They keep the action moving, and they keep you as a reader interested. Without the characters, you wouldn't have a story!

Goals

Here you'll learn how to:

✔ **tell the difference between major and minor characters**

✔ **find clues to help you understand characters**

✔ **see how characters change**

Before Reading

From the moment you open a book, pay attention to the characters in a story. Find out who the story is about. Most stories have two kinds of characters: major and minor.

Stories and Poems

Major Characters

Major, or main, characters are the ones in the story most often. What they do is very important to the plot. Their names are often in the title, and you may see pictures of them. Look at this passage. Who is the major character in this story?

> **from _Jake Drake Know-It-All_ by Andrew Clements**
>
> I'm Jake, Jake Drake. I'm in fourth grade, and I'm ten years old. And I have to tell the truth about something: I've been crazy about computers all my life.

Major character

You know right away that Jake Drake is the main character of this novel. He's telling the story.

Minor Characters

Most stories have many characters but only one or two major ones. The others are called minor characters. They're not as important to the plot. They also don't appear as much as the major characters do. You don't learn as much about a minor character as you do a major one.

When you read _Jake Drake Know-It-All_, you learn about several other characters. But it's Jake that this story is mainly about.

During Reading

You find out about characters just like you find out about real people. As you read, watch what they do. Listen to what they say. Notice how they look.

Read for Clues

Some characters directly tell you about themselves. But usually you have to look for clues about characters and then figure out what they mean. Pay attention to these clues:

■ what characters do, say, and think

■ how they look and how they treat others

■ what others say about them

What else do you learn about Jake here?

> **from Jake Drake Know-It-All**
>
> Like I said before, I'm ten now, so I've had some time to figure out some stuff. And one thing I know for sure is this: There's nothing worse than a know-it-all.
> Don't get me wrong. I'm pretty smart, and I like being smart. And almost all the kids I know, they're pretty smart, too.

What Jake feels

Stories and Poems

Now look at what happens when Jake tells his best friend they can't work together to win a prize.

Willie shrugged. "Okay. But if I win, I'll still let you use my computer sometimes, okay?"

I smiled and said, "Sure. That'll be great."

But inside, to myself, I said, *You? Win the science fair? Forget about it, Willie. That grand prize is* mine.

What Jake thinks

As you read a story, your opinion of a character can change. Jake doesn't seem so nice now, does he? Use a Character Map to collect details about characters.

Character Map

WHAT HE SAYS AND DOES	WHAT OTHERS THINK
• loves computers • doesn't like "know-it-alls"	• Willie wants to work with him.

JAKE DRAKE

HOW HE LOOKS AND FEELS	HOW I FEEL
• thinks most kids he knows are pretty smart • likes being smart	• seems kind of funny • should be nicer to his best friend

Look for Changes

In many stories and novels, major characters change. They might learn a lesson or change the way they act.

Watch for a change in Jake as you read more.

from Jake Drake Know-It-All

But, worst of all, back when Willie wanted to be my partner, what did I do? I sent him off on his own. I threw him into the shark tank with Kevin and into the snake pit with Marsha. Willie and I could have had fun working on a project. Together.

Jake is angry at himself.

Jake doesn't like the way he has acted. He knows he was mean to Willie. So he decides to work with Willie after all.

By the end of the book, Jake realizes two important lessons. First, he will never let himself be a know-it-all. Second, no prize is worth as much as a good friend.

Use a Character Change Chart to help you see the changes that characters go through. Look at the example for Jake on the next page.

Stories and Poems

Character Change Chart

BEGINNING	MIDDLE	END
• Jake wants to win the computer. • He doesn't want to work with Willie because he doesn't want to share the prize.	Jake tries to be a "know-it-all" just so he can win.	• Jake learns that it's better to work with someone than to win. • Jake and Willie stay great friends.

POSSIBLE THEME

Friendship is more important than winning a big prize.

Sometimes characters make mistakes and learn a lesson. Usually major characters find out something important about themselves and their lives. That's what happens to Jake.

A Character Change Chart helps you focus on what the major character is like in the beginning, middle, and end of a story. Filling in the chart can help you think about the theme—the author's message about life.

After Reading

After you finish reading a story or novel, take a few minutes to think about the major and minor characters.

■ Who are they? What are they like?

■ What do they do and say?

■ Do any characters change?

■ How do you feel about them?

CHARACTER CHANGE CHART

Look over your Character Map and Character Change Chart. If you don't understand or can't remember something about a character, go back and reread parts of the book. If you can, share your ideas and questions about the characters with a friend. As Jake Drake learned, "Two heads are better than one."

Summing Up

■ **Characters can be major or minor. You learn more about major characters, and they appear often.**

■ **Pay attention to what characters say, do, think, and feel and how other characters react to them.**

■ **Watch for changes in characters. These changes help you understand the theme, or author's message about life.**

Stories and Poems

Focus on Setting

When you read a story, you want to find out who's in it and what happens to them. But you also need to know *where* and *when* the story takes place. That's what setting means—the time and place of a story.

A story can be set anywhere and at any time. Some stories are set in the present. Others take place hundreds of years ago or even in the future.

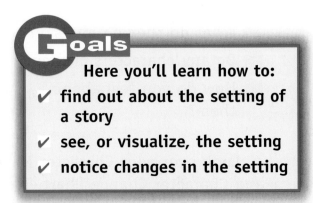

Goals

Here you'll learn how to:
- ✔ **find out about the setting of a story**
- ✔ **see, or visualize, the setting**
- ✔ **notice changes in the setting**

The setting is more than just description. It can be very important in a story. The setting can affect how the characters feel and what problems they face.

Before Reading

During your preview of a novel or story, look for words about place and time. In many stories, you can find out where and when the story takes place in the first few paragraphs.

Find Clues about Time

Look for words that tell you about the time. The words may be the hour, the day of the week, the month, or the season. Look for specific dates. Figure out if the story is set in the past or the present.

Below is a part of a novel called *Stone Fox*. When does the story take place?

> ### from *Stone Fox* by John Reynolds Gardiner
>
> Grandfather always got up real early in the morning. So early that it was still dark outside. He would make a fire. Then he would make breakfast and call little Willy. "Hurry up or you'll be eating with the chickens," he would say. Then he would throw his head back and laugh.
>
> Once little Willy went back to sleep. When he woke up, he found his plate out in the chicken coop. It was picked clean. He never slept late again after that.
>
> That is . . . until this morning. For some reason, Grandfather had forgotten to call him. That's when little Willy discovered that Grandfather was still in bed. There could be only one explanation. Grandfather was playing. It was another trick.

Details about time

Stories and Poems

What words tell you about the time? The words *breakfast* and *morning* tip you off to the time of day.

Find Clues about Place

Now look for clues about where this story takes place. Sometimes the place is named, and sometimes it's not. What can you find out about where Willy lives?

from *Stone Fox*

Little Willy lived with his grandfather on a small potato farm in Wyoming. It was hard work living on a potato farm, but it was also a lot of fun. Especially when Grandfather felt like playing.

Details about place

In this story, the place is the state of Wyoming. You also learn that the characters live on a small potato farm.

You may want to take notes on the setting. A Setting Chart is a good tool for keeping track of where and when a story takes place.

Setting Chart

TITLE Stone Fox	
CLUES ABOUT TIME	CLUES ABOUT PLACE
early morning when Grandfather stays in bed	small potato farm in Wyoming

During Reading

As you read, pay attention to the clues about time and place. Get a picture of the setting in your head. Try to notice when the setting changes.

Picture the Setting

The words that authors use to describe the setting help you form a picture in your mind. Read this description of a winter scene. Then draw a picture of it.

from Stone Fox

It's easy to tell when it's winter in Wyoming. There is snow on everything: the trees, the houses, the roads, the fields, and even the people, if they stay outside long enough.

Details of the scene

Picture

Stories and Poems

Look for Changes in the Setting

The setting of a story often changes. Stories can cover many months or even years. Events can start in one place and end up somewhere else.

Watch for changes in the setting as you read. A different setting can mean a change in a character or signal a change in the plot. For instance, at one point Willy has to get $500 to save his grandfather's farm. He decides to enter a dogsled race to win the money. The scene at the race surprises him.

> **from *Stone Fox***
>
> He couldn't believe what he saw.
> **New scene** — Main Street was jammed with people, lined up on both sides of the street. There were people on rooftops and people hanging out of windows. Little Willy hadn't expected such a big turnout. They must have all come to see Stone Fox.

Stone Fox has many changes in setting. It begins on a fall morning in a farmhouse in the country. But it ends in a busy town on a cold winter night when Willy enters the race.

After Reading

After you read a story, think about how the setting was important. You may want to make a quick list of the different settings to help you remember what happens where in a story. Write important details about the setting in Summary Notes. Here's an example.

> **Summary Notes**

WHERE AND WHEN
- on the farm in the fall
- in a store in the winter
- one night on Main Street

WHAT HAPPENS
- Grandfather gets sick.
- Willy needs money.
- Willy enters a dogsled race.

Summing Up

- The setting is the time and place of a story.
- Look for clues about the setting in the beginning of a story.
- Create a picture of the setting in your mind.
- Think about how and why the setting changes.

Stories and Poems

Elements of Literature

You probably have a few favorite stories and books. But can you explain *why* you like them? Knowing about the elements of literature helps you know why you like a book or story.

This part of the handbook explains the key terms used to talk about stories and poems.

Elements of Literature

Alliteration

When you read the poem below, what sounds do you hear repeated over and over?

EXAMPLE

"Flea Fur All" by Douglas Florian

Fur fills fleas with glee:
In fur they feel so fancy-free.
They prance and dance in ecstasy.
In cheetahs, chipmunks, and chimpanzees:
Fur fills fleas with glee.

Same beginning sounds

DESCRIPTION

Poets use **alliteration** when they repeat the same consonant sound at the beginnings of words. In the poem above, the *f* sound is repeated. Look at *fur, fills, fleas, feel, and fancy-free*. The **ch** sound is also repeated in *cheetahs, chipmunks,* and *chimpanzees*.

Hearing these same sounds over and over makes a poem more fun and interesting to read.

DEFINITION

Alliteration is the use of words with the same beginning consonant sound.

Stories and Poems

Characters

The people in stories are called characters. In some stories, animals, make-believe creatures, and even things can be characters. They talk, wear clothes, and go places. They act just like people.

EXAMPLE — from *The Stories Julian Tells* by Ann Cameron

My father is a big man with wild black hair. When he laughs, the sun laughs in the windowpanes. When he thinks, you can almost see his thoughts sitting on all the tables and chairs. When he is angry, me and my little brother, Huey, shiver to the bottom of our shoes.

> Three characters

> What the man looks like and does

DESCRIPTION

Characters take part in the action of a story. Some stories have many characters, and some have only a few. You can understand characters by paying attention to what they say and do, how they look and feel, and what other characters say about them.

DEFINITION

Characters are people, animals, make-believe creatures, or things that take part in the action of a story.

Dialogue

Listen to people talk. What they say can tell you a lot about them. That's true for real people and characters in stories. Read this dialogue. What do you think of the grandpa and the girl?

EXAMPLE

from *The Bee Tree*
by Patricia Polacco

"I'm tired of reading, Grampa."
Mary Ellen sighed. "I'd rather be
outdoors running and playing."
"So you don't feel like reading,
eh? Feel like running, do you? Then
I expect this is just the right time to
find a bee tree!" he said, taking down a
jar and putting on his lucky hat.

Quotes around the words a character says

New paragraph for a new speaker

Speech tags tell who's talking.

DESCRIPTION

Dialogue can tell you a lot about the characters and the action of a story. Most dialogue is put inside quotation marks.

Usually lines of dialogue have *speech tags*, such as "he said" or "Mary Ellen sighed." The speech tags show you which character says what. When a new character starts to talk, the author starts a new paragraph.

DEFINITION

Dialogue is the talking that characters do in a story.

Stories and Poems

329

Fiction

Stories come from an author's imagination. They are made up.

EXAMPLE from *Charlotte's Web* by E. B. White

At last, Wilbur saw the creature that had spoken to him in such a kindly way. Stretched across the upper part of the doorway was a big spiderweb, and hanging from the top of the web, head down, was a large grey spider. She was about the size of a gumdrop. She had eight legs, and she was waving one of them at Wilbur in friendly greeting. "See me now?" she asked.

Made-up characters

DESCRIPTION

Any made-up story is called **fiction**. Some fictional stories, such as ones about talking spiders and pigs, like *Charlotte's Web,* are clearly make-believe. Other stories may seem real, but the characters and the events are made up.

DEFINITION

Fiction is a story that is made up.

Imagery

Writers use details to make you really see and feel what they're describing. Can you see a picture in your mind as you read this poem?

EXAMPLE "Growing Old" by Rose Henderson

When I grow old I hope to be
As beautiful as Grandma Lee.
Her hair is soft and fluffy white.
Her eyes are blue and candle bright.
And down her cheeks are cunning piles
Of little ripples when she smiles.

Details of what she looks like

DESCRIPTION

Poets like to use words that appeal to your five senses—sight, hearing, smell, taste, and touch. This kind of language that appeals to the senses is called **imagery.** The words used to describe Grandma Lee create a clear picture, or image, in your head.

As you read, note the imagery writers create with vivid details.

DEFINITION

Imagery is language that helps you see, hear, feel, smell, or taste something described.

Stories and Poems

Metaphor

Writers often like to compare one thing to another. Comparing helps you see things in new ways. Can you tell what is compared in this poem?

EXAMPLE

"When I Was Lost" by Dorothy Aldis

Underneath my belt
My stomach was a stone.
Sinking was the way I felt.
And hollow.
And Alone.

> A stomach is compared to a stone.

DESCRIPTION

A **metaphor** compares two things. It says one thing *is* or *was* the other thing. In the example, the poet says her stomach was a stone. This is a metaphor.

Writers use metaphors to make you think about something in a new way. Did you ever think of a stomach as a stone? What do a stomach and a stone have in common?

DEFINITION

A **metaphor** compares two things. Usually it says one thing is something else.

Mood

Stories and poems can make you feel sad, happy, surprised, or angry. How do you feel while you're reading this passage below?

EXAMPLE

from Fantastic Mr. Fox by Roald Dahl

The animals froze. They stayed absolutely still, their ears pricked, their bodies tense. Then they heard the sound of a door being opened. The door was at the top of a flight of stone steps leading down from the house to the cellar.

And now someone was starting to come down those steps.

Details that create a scary, nervous feeling

DESCRIPTION

The feeling that a story gives you is called the **mood.** The mood might be peaceful, sad, or scary. Here the author uses words such as *froze* and *tense* to create a scary mood.

Did you feel nervous or a little frightened while reading this? That's exactly what the author wanted!

DEFINITION

The mood of a story is how it makes you feel.

Stories and Poems

Narrator

All stories are told by someone. As you read a story, notice who is telling it. Here are two examples.

EXAMPLE  from *Squanto's Journey* by Joseph Bruchac

My story is both strange and true. I was born in the year the English call 1590. My family were leaders of the Patuxet people and I, too, was raised to lead. But in 1614 I was taken to Spain against my will. Now it is 1621 and I am again in my homeland. My name is Squanto. I would like to tell you my tale.

> **First-person narrator**

DESCRIPTION

The **narrator** is the person who tells the story. In some stories, the narrator is also a character in the story.

In this example, Squanto tells about what happened to him. He is a *first-person narrator*. The words *I*, *my*, and *me* are clues that a story has a first-person narrator.

Now read another story. Who is telling it?

EXAMPLE

from *Sideways Stories from Wayside School* by Louis Sachar

Mrs. Gorf had a long tongue and pointed ears. She was the meanest teacher in Wayside School. She taught the class on the thirtieth story.

"If you children are bad," she warned, "or if you answer a problem wrong, I'll wiggle my ears, stick out my tongue, and turn you into apples!" Mrs. Gorf didn't like children, but she loved apples.

> Third-person narrator

DESCRIPTION

Some stories are told by someone who is not in the story. In this example, Mrs. Gorf is not telling her own story. Someone else—the author—is telling about Mrs. Gorf and her class. This story has a *third-person narrator*. It's easy to tell when a story has a third-person narrator. The writer uses the pronouns *he, his, she,* and *they* to refer to the characters.

DEFINITION

The **narrator** is the person who tells the story. A *first-person narrator* tells his or her own story. A *third-person narrator* tells a story about someone else.

Stories and Poems

335

Onomatopoeia

Some words sound more like noises than words. Look for words like that in the poem below.

EXAMPLE

"Pie Problem" by
Shel Silverstein

If I eat one more piece of pie, I'll die!
If I can't have one more piece of pie, I'll die!
So since it's all decided I must die,
I might as well have one more piece of pie.
MMMM—OOOH—MY!
Chomp—Gulp—'Bye.

Words that sound like
what they mean

DESCRIPTION

Words that sound like the noises they describe are called **onomatopoeia.** When you *chomp* on a mouthful of potato chips, the noise it makes sounds like *chomp*! And when you *gulp* down a glass of milk, your throat makes a *gulp* sound. *Mmmm* and *oooh* also describe sounds.

Authors use onomatopoeia to make their writing fun to read and hear.

DEFINITION

Onomatopoeia means using words that sound like the noises they name.

Personification

Lots of stories and poems have things that act and seem like real people. For example, what is Summer doing in the poem below?

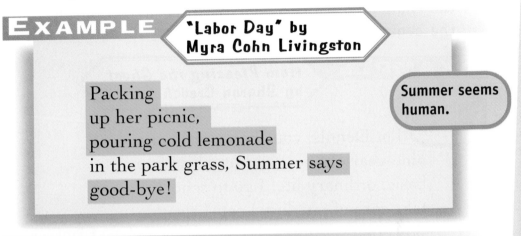

EXAMPLE "Labor Day" by Myra Cohn Livingston

Packing
up her picnic,
pouring cold lemonade
in the park grass, Summer says
good-bye!

Summer seems human.

DESCRIPTION

Making something that isn't human seem human is called **personification.** In this poem, Summer acts like a person. She packs up her picnic, pours out the cold lemonade, and says good-bye.

Of course, seasons can't really do any of these things! The poet makes summertime seem human to make you think about the season in a new and unusual way.

DEFINITION

Personification is making a thing seem like a person. Authors can make animals, objects, and ideas speak, move, wear clothes, and have feelings.

Stories and Poems

Plot

In stories, something usually happens. Characters make decisions, go places, and do things. Sometimes things happen that surprise the characters. For example, what is happening in the beginning of this story?

EXAMPLE

from *Pleasing the Ghost*
by Sharon Creech

Main character

I'm Dennis, your basic, ordinary nine-year-old boy, and usually I live a basic, ordinary life. I go to school, I take care of my dog, I eat, I sleep. Sometimes, though, my life is not so ordinary. This is because of the ghosts.

Problem

DESCRIPTION

The action of a story is called the **plot.** In the example, Dennis hints that his problem is ghosts. What will happen next? What will Dennis do? What happens and what the characters in a story do make up the plot.

A plot is made up of three main parts.

Beginning → **Middle** → **End**

Parts of a Plot

When you read a story or novel, look for these three parts.

1. Beginning

In the first part of most stories, authors give you background. They tell you about the setting and the main character. You often find out about a problem the character has.

2. Middle

This is when the characters try to figure out and solve the problem. Tension usually builds to a turning point, called the climax.

3. End

In the last part of the story, everything starts to work out. The author explains how the characters solved the problem.

DEFINITION

A **plot** of a story is the action, or what happens to the characters.

Stories and Poems

Poetry

Poems are a special kind of writing. They can be long or short, serious or silly. What do you think of this poem about a girl in a library?

EXAMPLE

**"At the Library"
by Nikki Grimes**

Words that rhyme

I flip the pages of a book and slip inside,
where crystal seas await and pirates hide.
I find a paradise where birds can talk,
where children fly and trees prefer to walk.
Sometimes I end up on a city street.
I recognize the brownskin girl I meet.
She's skinny, but she's strong, and brave,
   and wise.
I smile because I see *me* in her eyes.

DESCRIPTION

Poetry looks different from stories. Poems say a lot in a few words. Poets often use rhymes, images, and rhythm to get across a feeling or idea.

Poetry also says things in special or surprising ways. It helps you think about things in new ways and often stirs up your feelings.

DEFINITION

Poetry is a special kind of writing. It expresses thoughts and feelings in an unusual way. It often uses rhythm and rhyme.

Rhyme

Poets often choose words so a poem sounds a certain way. Do you like how this poem sounds?

EXAMPLE

"Noodles" by Janet S. Wong

Noodles for breakfast,
Noodles for lunch,
Noodles for dinner,
Noodles that crunch,
Noodles to twirl,
Noodles to slurp —
I could eat noodles
all day! Burp!

> Rhyming words

DESCRIPTION

Words that **rhyme** sound the same at the end. In the poem above, *lunch* and *crunch* rhyme. So do *slurp* and *burp*. In many poems, you can find the rhyming words at the ends of lines.

Poets use rhyme to add a musical sound to their poems. Rhyme makes poems more fun and interesting to read.

DEFINITION

Rhyme is the same sounds at the ends of two or more words.

Stories and Poems

Rhythm

Poems have a rhythm, or beat, just like music. Read the poem below. Can you tap out a beat as you go?

EXAMPLE

"The Locked Closet" by Jeff Moss

There's a closet where nobody goes.
What is lurking inside no one knows.
Like a body that's dead,
Or a weird shrunken head,
Or my mother's old high school prom
   clothes.

Note the beat when you say the lines.

DESCRIPTION

This short poem is easy to read out loud and fun to hear. The regular beat you can hear in the lines is called **rhythm.**

The rhythm comes from how the poet arranges the words. The highlighted parts in the example show what you stress, or say extra loudly, when you read each line. The poet has chosen word parts, or syllables, that are stressed in a regular pattern.

DEFINITION

Rhythm is the pattern of sounds and beats you can hear in the lines of a poem.

Setting

Read the passage below. Can you tell where the story takes place?

EXAMPLE

from *Encyclopedia Brown and the Case of the Treasure Hunt* by Donald J. Sobol

Idaville looked like an ordinary seaside town. It had clean beaches, two delicatessens, and three movie theaters. It had churches, a synagogue, four banks, and a Little League.

What made Idaville different from anyplace in the world was a redbrick house on Rover Avenue. For there lived ten-year-old Encyclopedia Brown, America's Sherlock Holmes in sneakers.

Place

DESCRIPTION

The **setting** of a story is where and when it takes place. Authors usually give you clues about the setting in the very beginning of a story. In this example, you learn about the town of Idaville. You also find out that Encyclopedia Brown lives in a brick house on Rover Avenue.

DEFINITION

The **setting** is where and when a story takes place.

Stories and Poems

Simile

Authors often compare one thing to another using the words *like* or *as*. Read this poem, which is full of comparisons to animals.

EXAMPLE **"I'm Roaring like a Lion"**
by Jack Prelutsky

I'm roaring like a lion,
I'm croaking like a frog,
I'm shrieking like a monkey,   **Six comparisons**
I'm grunting like a hog.

I'm snorting like a buffalo,
I'm whooping like a crane.
My mother's making liver . . .
I thought I should complain.

DESCRIPTION

In a **simile,** a writer compares two things using the words *like* or *as*. Similes are word pictures. They help you see things differently. The poem above compares the sounds an unhappy person makes to the sounds of six different animals. Using similes like these can make it fun to read a poem.

DEFINITION

A **simile** makes a comparison between two things using the words *like* or *as*.

Stanza

Poems don't use paragraphs, but they often group lines together. This poem, for example, has two parts.

EXAMPLE   **"Many People Who Are Smart" by Karla Kuskin**

Many people who are smart
in physics, French, and math and art
cannot tell two bugs apart.

Two stanzas

❶

Bugs are not very smart
in math or physics, French or art,
But they can tell two bugs apart.

❷

DESCRIPTION

The two groups of lines above are called **stanzas.** Stanzas may have two, three, or more lines each. Using stanzas helps poets organize their ideas.

When you see a new stanza begin, it usually means the poet is moving to a different image, thought, or idea. Two stanzas make sense for this poem. It talks about two different things: people and bugs.

DEFINITION

A stanza is a group of lines in a poem. Each stanza usually is about one image, thought, or idea.

Stories and Poems

Style

Writers have different ways of writing. They do it by putting together words and sentences in different ways. Do you like the way this story is written?

EXAMPLE — from *The Great Kapok Tree* by Lynne Cherry

The man looked about and saw the sun streaming through the canopy. Spots of bright light glowed like jewels amidst the dark green forest. Strange and beautiful plants seemed to dangle in the air, suspended from the great Kapok tree.

Hard words

Long sentence

The man smelled the fragrant perfume of their flowers. He felt the steamy mist rising from the forest floor. But he heard no sound, for the creatures were strangely silent.

Details of sights, sounds, and smells

DESCRIPTION

An author's **style** is his or her own special way of writing. You wear your hair or dress in a certain style. Writers also write in a specific style. The kinds of sentences and words the author uses make up his or her style. What can you say about the style of the passage above?

DEFINITION

Style is the author's way of putting together words and sentences.

Theme

Most stories have a theme, or main idea. What is the main idea in the passage below?

EXAMPLE

from *Spotlight on Cody*
by **Betsy Duffey**

The spotlight focused on P.J. now instead of him. He realized something then. When the spotlight is on you, you can't see anyone else—and he didn't like that. But he loved the warm glow he had felt when everyone had seen the picture *he* had drawn. Everyone's talents were different. From singing to dancing. From the Hokey Pokey to the Macarena. From making a movie to making a poster. Just like his dad had said, everyone has a best thing to share.

The author's point

DESCRIPTION

A **theme** is the main idea or ideas that the author wants to get across in a story. Sometimes a character will say what the theme is. Other times the author will give you clues to put together. In the passage above, you see that P.J. has realized something important about life. He realizes that everyone has a special talent to share. This is the theme of the story.

DEFINITION

The **theme** in a story is the main point or message about life.

Stories and Poems

Reading for
Tests

Reading a Test and Test Questions

Focus on Tests

Focus on Reading Tests
Focus on Language Tests
Focus on Writing Tests
Focus on Math Tests

Reading a Test and Test Questions

How do you feel on the morning of a test? Do you worry? If so, you're not alone. Very few people like taking tests. Almost everybody gets a little bit nervous before a test.

But tests don't *have* to make you feel that way. A few good tips may help you relax before tests and improve your scores.

Goals

Here you'll learn how to:

✔ **prepare for different tests and test questions**

✔ **use the strategy of skimming to find answers**

Before Reading

First, remember to get ready for the test you're about to take. If you know a test is coming up, try doing three things.

■ Find out what the test will be like.

■ Find any books or papers you need to study. Study a little every day.

■ Go to sleep early the night before a test.

A Set a Purpose

For any test you're taking, your reading purpose is the same.

- **What is the test question asking?**
- **What information do I need to answer it?**

B Preview

When your teacher hands you the test, take a deep breath. Begin previewing the test. Try to get a sense of what the questions are like. Look for these items:

Preview Checklist

✔ directions

✔ main parts of the test

✔ kinds of readings and questions

✔ how much time you have

During your preview, you may see questions that will be easy to answer. You may want to mark these with a star. They are the questions you'll want to answer first.

Now try using this checklist for previewing a test. Preview the reading test on the next page.

Tests

Directions: Read "The Boatman." Then answer the questions. You have 40 minutes.

The Boatman (A Middle Eastern Folktale)

A rich man asked a boatman to row him across the river. But the journey was long and slow, and the man grew bored. He began a conversation.

"Boatman," he said, "let us pass the time by speaking of interesting matters. Have you studied math or grammar?"

"No," replied the boatman. "I've no use for those tools."

"What a pity," snickered the rich man. "You've wasted half your life! It is useful to know these subjects!"

Suddenly, the boat hit a sharp rock in the middle of the river and began to fill with water. The boatman turned to the rich man and said, "Pardon my dim and simple mind. But sir, tell me, have you ever learned to swim?"

"No!" bragged the rich man. "I've spent my time thinking."

"In that case," smiled the boatman, "you've wasted *all* your life. Alas, the boat is sinking!"

Reading Test, continued

Directions: Read each question and decide which answer is correct. Circle the letter of the correct answer. If you don't know an answer, make the best guess you can.

PREVIEW

Directions

1. The rich man begins the conversation because he . . .
   A. is polite.
   B. wants to learn about boating.
   C. is sick.
   D. is bored.

PREVIEW

Three multiple-choice questions

2. In the end, how does the boatman feel about the rich man?
   A. He likes him a lot.
   B. He wants to be like him.
   C. He makes fun of him.
   D. He is worried about him.

3. Which sentence best tells the lesson of "The Boatman"?
   A. Always learn to swim.
   B. Bragging gets you nowhere.
   C. Boats are not safe.
   D. Don't ask questions.

Tests

C Plan

Maybe you noticed these details about the test.

- The test is 40 minutes long.
- The reading is a story about two people.
- All three questions are multiple-choice.

After your preview, plan your time. You may want to mark important words in the questions. Then, to answer them, you will need to go back to parts of the reading to look for answers. Here the strategy of skimming can help.

Reading Strategy: Skimming

When you skim, you move your eyes quickly over the page. Look for key words and phrases. Don't read every sentence word for word. Sometimes it helps to run your finger down the middle of the page when you skim. Stop only when you see a key word that relates to one of the test questions.

During Reading

Previewing a test takes only a minute or two. Most of your time will be spent reading, skimming, and answering questions.

D Read with a Purpose

Remember that your purpose is to answer each question correctly. Before you can do that, however, you need to understand the reading passage.

Read the Passage

Do a careful reading of the story. You always have to do that. Try not to rush through it.

- Look for key words and phrases that match the key words in the questions.
- If you can write on the test, circle important details.
- Keep asking yourself, "What is the author saying here?"

Read the Questions

Remember that every word in a question is important, so read carefully. Take your time. Be sure you know what information you need to find.

Now take a closer look at the sample questions. The first one is a fact question. That means the answer is "right there" in the reading. Find the key words in the first question.

Tests

1. The rich man begins the conversation
because he . . .
   A. is polite.
   B. wants to learn about boating.
   C. is sick.
   D. is bored.

Answer Fact Questions

To find an answer to a fact question like this one, return to the reading. Skim for the same key words highlighted in the question. Then read one sentence before and one sentence after the key words.

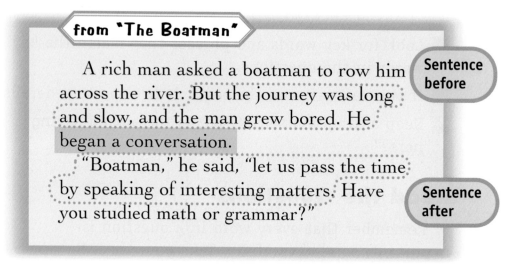

from "The Boatman"

A rich man asked a boatman to row him across the river. But the journey was long and slow, and the man grew bored. He began a conversation.

"Boatman," he said, "let us pass the time by speaking of interesting matters. Have you studied math or grammar?"

Sentence before

Sentence after

You can easily find the part where the rich man first talks. Look at the sentence right before the key words "began a conversation." It tells why he starts to talk. The correct answer to Question 1 is **D**.

Answer Critical Thinking Questions

The answer to critical thinking questions is not "right there" in the text. Inference questions are a common kind of critical thinking question. For these questions, take information from the reading and put it together with what you already know.

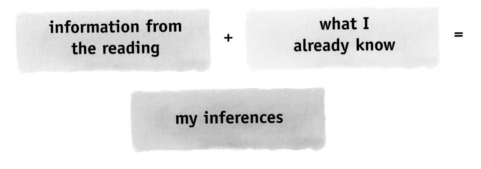

information from the reading	+	what I already know	=

my inferences

Now look again at Question 2 on the test. Reread the question, and highlight key words.

from **Reading Test**

2. In the end, how does the boatman feel about the rich man?

Key words

    A. He likes him a lot.
    B. He wants to be like him.
    C. He makes fun of him.
    D. He is worried about him.

Next, read the answer choices. Read them all even if you're sure you know which one is correct. Then return to the passage. Skim the end where the boatman says the boat is sinking. Look for clues about the boatman's feelings toward the rich man.

Tests

The boatman turned to the rich man and said, "Pardon my dim and simple mind. But sir, tell me, have you ever learned to swim?"

Clues

"No!" bragged the rich man. "I've spent my time thinking."

"In that case," smiled the boatman, "you've wasted *all* your life. Alas, the boat is sinking!"

Look at the highlighted clues in the reading. Then return to the four answer choices. Decide which one makes the most sense. Right away you can rule out answers **A** and **B**. The boatman tells the rich man he's wasted his life. That's not something you say to a friend or someone you want to be like. Talk through the last two answers to yourself.

Think Aloud

I don't think the boatman is worried. He smiles at the end. That makes me think he's making fun of the rich man. C is correct.

E Connect

If you connect to a reading, you can understand it better. To make your connections, ask yourself, "How do I feel about this reading? What does it remind me of?" For example, look at the connection a reader made here.

from "The Boatman"

"What a pity," snickered the rich man. "You've wasted half your life! It is useful to know these subjects!"

That's a mean thing to say.

By making a connection to what you read, you can understand it better. By thinking about how you would feel, you know what the rich man is really like.

After Reading

Use the last few minutes of the test to check your answers.

F Pause and Reflect

As you check your work, ask yourself questions about the test.

- Did I understand what each question is asking?
- Did I answer each question the best I can?
- Is there anything I need to spend more time on?

Tests

ⓖ Reread

If you have time, return to the test questions you think you got right. Be sure you marked the answers correctly.

You also need to go back to any questions you weren't able to answer. Reread them. Think again about what they are asking. For example, look again at the third question.

from Reading Test

Key word

3. Which sentence best tells the lesson of "The Boatman"?
   A. Always learn to swim.
   B. Bragging gets you nowhere.
   C. Boats are not safe.
   D. Don't ask questions.

Think aloud to yourself. Talk your way through the question.

Think Aloud

The boatman tells the rich man he has wasted his life. The boatman thinks the rich man shouldn't brag so much. The author even uses <u>bragged</u> in the story. The answer is B. The other answers don't fit as well with the story's ending.

H Remember

You're done with a test when you hand it in. But it's a good idea to think about it for a while longer, even after you've turned it in.

■ Ask your friends how they answered the questions. How did their answers compare to yours?

■ When you get your test back, look over any questions you missed. You never know when you'll see the same sort of questions again.

Summing Up

When you read a test, use the reading process. Use the strategy of **skimming** to find answers to fact questions.

For critical thinking questions, put together what you found in the reading with your own ideas and experiences. Check that all your answers are clear and easy to read.

Tests

361

Focus on Reading Tests

The purpose of a reading test is to check your ability to read, understand, and react to a story or article.

Most reading tests contain two kinds of readings—fiction and nonfiction. Often the nonfiction readings seem hard because they ask you for specific facts or about main ideas.

Fact questions ask you to find information that's directly stated in the reading. Critical thinking questions ask you to pick out main ideas and put together facts from the reading with what you already know. In this lesson, you'll learn how to respond to both kinds of questions.

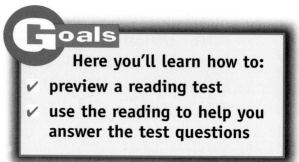

Goals

Here you'll learn how to:
- ✔ **preview a reading test**
- ✔ **use the reading to help you answer the test questions**

Before Reading

To do your best on a reading test, be sure to prepare and preview.

CRITICAL THINKING

CRITICAL THINKING

FACT

Prepare

How can you prepare for a test you've never seen before? Here are a few suggestions.

▪ **Listen.** First, find out what you can about the test.

▪ **Practice.** Ask your teacher for some example questions. Try to answer them.

▪ **Get Ready.** Get a good night's sleep the night before the test.

Preview

As soon as your teacher hands you the test, begin previewing. Look quickly at the reading and the questions that go with it. Watch for these items:

▪ directions
▪ title of the reading passage
▪ kind of reading— fiction or nonfiction
▪ first and last sentences
▪ number and kinds of questions

Now preview part of a reading test. What do you notice on your preview?

Tests

Directions: Read the passage. Then answer the questions that follow.

from "Killer Whales"

The orca, or killer whale, gets its name because it is a good hunter. Killer whales can swim fast. They use their sharp teeth to eat fish, squid, seals, and birds. They have even attacked dolphins and other large whales. Their only enemy is human beings.

Killer whales are super big. They can grow to be 27 feet long and weigh up to 12,000 pounds. An average killer whale eats more than 500 pounds of food a day!

1. Which of these sentences is <u>not</u> true of killer whales?
     A. They are fast swimmers.
     B. Sometimes they eat birds.
     C. They have no teeth.
     D. Humans are their enemy.
2. What is the main idea in "Killer Whales"?
     A. Killer whales are big.
     B. Killer whales are powerful hunters.
     C. Killer whales eat lots of different things.
     D. Killer whales live a long time.

During Reading

After you preview, begin reading the article on whales. If you can, make a few notes on the test. Highlight or circle key words in each question.

Read the Passage

Every reading is different. Still, most nonfiction readings have a few things in common. Here are some tips to try.

- Look at the title. It may tell the subject.
- Pay extra attention to the first sentence of each paragraph.
- Look for repeated words. If the author mentions it more than once, it's probably important.

Read the Questions

Once you finish the reading, you're ready to answer the questions. Read the first question again. Look for key words in it. What do you need to find out?

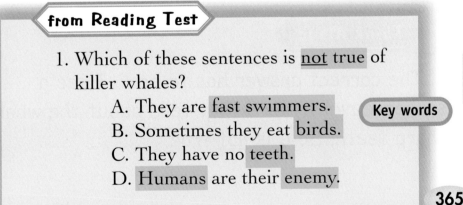

from Reading Test

1. Which of these sentences is <u>not</u> true of killer whales?
   A. They are fast swimmers.
   B. Sometimes they eat birds.
   C. They have no teeth.
   D. Humans are their enemy.

Key words

Tests

365

Find the Answers

Tests on nonfiction often ask you for small details. It's hard to remember everything after one reading. You'll have to go back and skim.

To find an answer to a fact question, return to the reading. Find key words that are in the question. Then read the sentence around the key words. The answer will probably be "right there" in the reading.

from "Killer Whales"

The orca, or killer whale, gets its name because it is a good hunter. Killer whales can swim fast. They use their sharp teeth to eat fish, squid, seals, and birds. They have even attacked dolphins and other large whales. Their only enemy is human beings.

Key words

After you have found the key words, test each possible answer. Read each answer choice carefully. Remember that the question asks you to find the sentence that is *not* true.

Think Aloud

The correct answer has to be C. I see a sentence right there that tells about the whale's sharp teeth. So C is <u>not</u> true.

Draw Conclusions

To answer critical thinking questions, you'll need to draw conclusions about the reading. To do that, you need to draw on your own ideas and experience.

Look again at Question 2.

from Reading Test

> 2. What is the main idea in "Killer Whales"? **Key words**
>
>   A. Killer whales are big.
>   B. Killer whales are powerful hunters.
>   C. Killer whales eat lots of different things.
>   D. Killer whales live a long time.

To answer this question, you need to know what a main idea is. Look at all four choices. Choose the one that tells a main idea. Thinking aloud can help.

Think Aloud

The main idea needs to cover <u>everything</u>. So A and C can't be true. D can't be right. The reading says nothing about how long the whales live. That means B must be correct.

Tests

After Reading

Always try to leave at least five minutes at the end of the test to check your answers.

▮ Go back to the questions that you thought were easiest. Be sure you marked the right answer.

▮ Take a second look at the hard questions. Try once more to answer these.

▮ Be sure you haven't skipped any questions.

Summing Up

■ Use the reading process to help you understand the nonfiction readings on a test and the questions about them.

■ To answer fact questions, return to the reading. Skim for key words from the question. Read the sentences around the key words.

■ For critical thinking questions, think about the main idea, and draw conclusions about what you read.

■ After the test, check your answers.

Focus on Language Tests

You will probably take language tests in school. They will test how well you can follow the rules for speaking and writing English. You can expect questions about capital letters, punctuation, and spelling. You may also answer questions about vocabulary, grammar, and using the library.

Using the reading process can help you do your best on language tests.

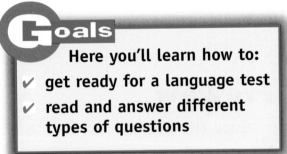

Goals

Here you'll learn how to:
- ✔ get ready for a language test
- ✔ read and answer different types of questions

Before Reading

Get a good night's sleep before the test. Once you get the test, take a few minutes to look it over.

Tests

Prepare

The best way to get ready for a language test is to keep up with what's going on in class. Ask questions in class about things you don't understand. Here are two other useful tips.

Listen. First, find out about the test you're about to take. Ask what kinds of questions will be on the test.

Study. Review any quizzes or worksheets you've done. Then review the pages you've covered in your textbook.

Preview

Once the test begins, do a quick preview. Watch for these items:

time limit

how to mark answers

different kinds of questions

For practice, preview the language test on the next page.

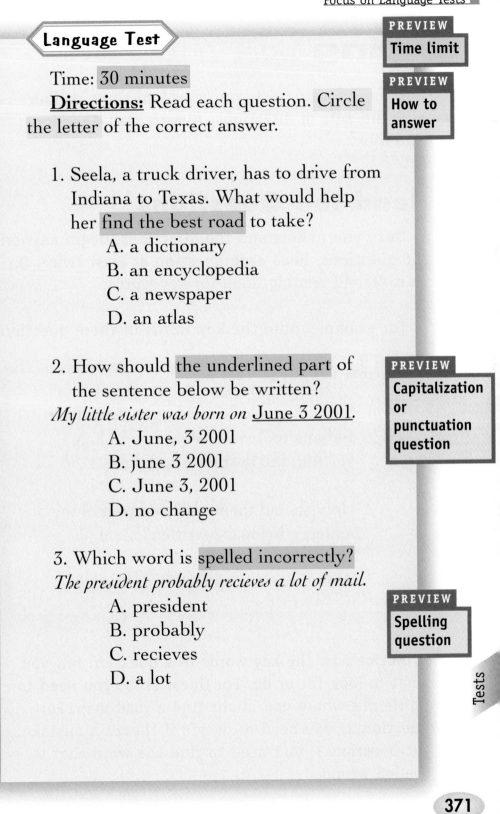

PREVIEW
Time limit

Language Test

Time: 30 minutes
Directions: Read each question. Circle
the letter of the correct answer.

PREVIEW
How to answer

1. Seela, a truck driver, has to drive from
   Indiana to Texas. What would help
   her find the best road to take?
   A. a dictionary
   B. an encyclopedia
   C. a newspaper
   D. an atlas

2. How should the underlined part of
   the sentence below be written?
   My little sister was born on <u>June 3 2001</u>.
   A. June, 3 2001
   B. june 3 2001
   C. June 3, 2001
   D. no change

PREVIEW
Capitalization or punctuation question

3. Which word is spelled incorrectly?
   The president probably recieves a lot of mail.
   A. president
   B. probably
   C. recieves
   D. a lot

PREVIEW
Spelling question

Tests

371

During Reading

On a language test, you may find three or four different sets of directions. Always read directions carefully.

Read the Questions

Once you understand the directions, begin answering the questions. Read each question at least twice. On your second reading, look for key words.

For example, note the key words in these questions.

> **from Language Test**
>
> **Key words**
>
> 1. Seela, a truck driver, has to drive from Indiana to Texas. What would help her find the best road to take?
>
> 2. How should the underlined part of the sentence below be written?
>
> 3. Which word is spelled incorrectly?

Notice how the key words in a question tell you what to look for or do. For Question 1, you need to figure out where you might find a road map. For Question 2, you need to decide if there's a mistake. For Question 3, you need to find the word that is spelled wrong.

Read the Answers

Sometimes you may think you know the answer to a question. But it's always a good idea to read through all of the answers. Read each answer choice carefully. Rule out any answers you know are wrong. Then see if you can spot the correct one. Look at this example.

> **from Language Test**
>
> 1. Seela, a truck driver, has to drive from Indiana to Texas. What would help her find the best road to take?
>   A. a dictionary
>   B. an encyclopedia
>   C. a newspaper
>   D. an atlas
>
> *I know A and C are not right.*

Crossing out **A** and **C** makes the question easier. That leaves two choices. **D** seems like the correct answer. An atlas is a book of maps. Now try the next one.

> **from Language Test**
>
> 2. How should the underlined part of the sentence below be written?
> *My little sister was born on* <u>June 3 2001</u>.
>   A. June, 3 2001
>   B. june 3 2001
>   C. June 3, 2001
>   D. no change
>
> *I know you need a comma somewhere. I think C is correct.*

Tests

373

Be Test Smart

Sometimes you'll come across test questions that seem super hard. When that happens, you still have to choose an answer. You may not know for sure if it's right. But remember to make a smart guess.

When you make a smart guess, you choose the answer that is *most likely* correct. Talk yourself through the question. Here is an example.

from Language Test

3. Which word is spelled incorrectly?
The president probably recieves a lot of mail.

Think Aloud

This question is hard. I feel like <u>probably</u> and <u>recieves</u> are both spelled incorrectly. But I'm going to guess <u>recieves</u> is wrong. It looks stranger to me than <u>probably</u>. I think <u>receives</u> might be the correct spelling.

Choosing the most likely answer is one way to be "test smart." Another tip is to watch for the words *only, never, not,* and *except.* They can change the meaning of the whole question.

After Reading

Always take the last five minutes to double-check your work.

- Look for questions you skipped over.
- Keep an eye out for careless errors.
- Be sure you marked the correct answer clearly.
- If you have time, go back to the hard questions. Ask yourself, "Does my answer still make sense?"

Summing Up

- **The best way to get ready for a language test is to keep up with your class work.**
- **On the day of the test, preview the test.**
- **Always read the question and all the answer choices carefully.**
- **Make a smart guess if you're not sure of an answer.**

Tests

375

Focus on Writing Tests

Soon you will start taking writing tests in school. Sometimes, you will write a story about your life. Other times, you'll be asked to write about a person, place, thing, or idea.

Writing tests show how well you know rules and strategies of good writing. In this lesson, you'll learn how to use the reading process to help you do well on writing tests.

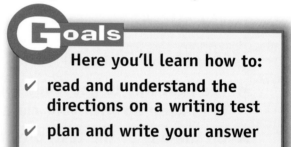

Goals

Here you'll learn how to:
- ✔ **read and understand the directions on a writing test**
- ✔ **plan and write your answer**

Before Reading

You might get nervous before a writing test. But writing tests are not that hard, as long as you're prepared.

Prepare

Here are three important tips to help you get ready for a writing test.

- **Listen.** First, find out as much as you can about what you will have to write.
- **Practice.** Ask your teacher to see sample writing tests. That way you'll know what kind of writing you need to do.
- **Plan.** Think ahead about what you'll do when you get the test.

Preview

On the day of the test, begin with a preview. Take a minute to see what's on the test. Look for these items:

- how much time you have to write
- type of writing you need to do
- topic of the writing
- what you will be graded on

Tests

During Reading

Reading the directions on a writing test is really important. It can be almost as important as the writing. Watch for the *type* of writing you need to do and the *topic*.

Writing Test

Directions: Everybody loves a party! Write how to plan a really great birthday party. Write at least one paragraph. When you finish, proofread your work.

Did you figure out what the directions are asking for? Now read them a second time. Look for key words that tell you what to do.

Writing Test

Key words

Directions: Everybody loves a party! Write ① how to ② plan a really great birthday party. Write ③ at least one paragraph. When you finish, ④ proofread your work.

① **kind of writing**—"how to" do something
② **topic**—planning a great birthday party
③ **length**—at least one paragraph
④ **proofreading**—checking your writing for errors

Make a Plan

Next, plan what you will say. Think for a minute before you start to write. Make a few notes. Use a graphic organizer that you can refer to as you write. Here is an example.

Process Notes

PLANNING A BIRTHDAY PARTY

1. Decide who, when, and where.

2. Write invitations.

3. Get everything ready.

4. Help everybody have fun.

Choose an organizer that works with the writing you're going to do. Process Notes are a perfect choice for a how-to paragraph.

Write Your Answer

Once you have your plan in place, you can begin writing. Start with a sentence that tells your main idea. Then explain the steps in your own words. Use signal words, such as *first, second, next, then,* and *last.* They will help your reader follow what you're saying.

PLANNING A BIRTHDAY PARTY

There are four steps you need to follow to plan a good party. First, decide who to invite and when and where to have the party. Second, write and send out the invitations. The third step is to get everything you need and then to set it all up. That means food, balloons, and games. Make everything look nice! Last, help everybody have fun.

Topic sentence

Signal words

1. **Topic sentence**—This tells what the essay is about.
2. **Signal words**—These words help the reader track what you are saying.

After Reading

When you're all done, go back and read what you wrote. Be sure your writing is clear and easy to read. Ask yourself, "Does what I wrote make sense? Does it seem too long or too short?" If you have a few minutes left at the end of a test, use it to check your writing.

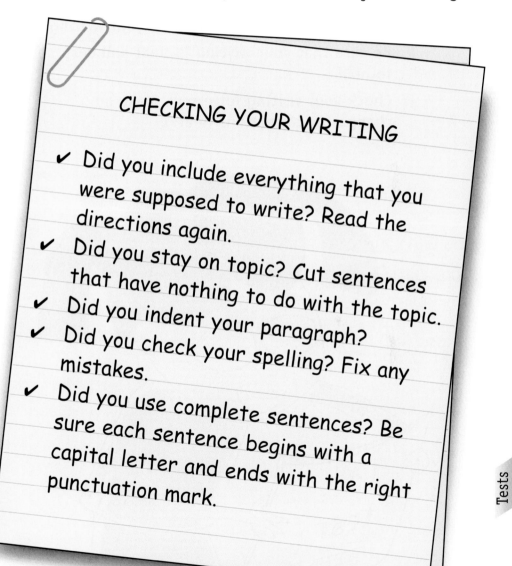

CHECKING YOUR WRITING

✔ Did you include everything that you were supposed to write? Read the directions again.

✔ Did you stay on topic? Cut sentences that have nothing to do with the topic.

✔ Did you indent your paragraph?

✔ Did you check your spelling? Fix any mistakes.

✔ Did you use complete sentences? Be sure each sentence begins with a capital letter and ends with the right punctuation mark.

Tests

Summing Up

- Preview the test. Be sure you know the type of writing you need to do and the topic you need to write about.

- Read the directions carefully and more than once.

- Use a graphic organizer to plan your writing.

- Be sure that your writing is clear and easy to read.

- Check your writing for errors. Make any changes or corrections neatly.

Focus on Math Tests

Did you know that being a good reader can help you do well on math tests? The reason is simple. Reading a math problem carefully is a key to solving it. The reading process gives you the tools and strategies to help you read carefully.

Goals

Here you'll learn how to:
- ✔ **prepare for and preview a math test**
- ✔ **read and understand math questions**

Before Reading

You need more than luck to do well on a math test. To do well, you must be prepared. Before you even answer the first question, you can do a lot.

First, be sure to read your math book. It will have example problems and terms you need to know. Work all of the practice problems, too. They are probably just like the ones you'll see on quizzes and tests.

Tests

Prepare

Here are some tips to help you get ready for a math test or quiz.

- **Listen.** Pay attention in class. Find out what the test or quiz will cover.
- **Practice.** Ask your teacher for sample problems. Solve as many practice problems as you can.
- **Study.** Skim the chapters in your textbook again and look over your old tests and worksheets.

Preview

When test time arrives, relax. Take the time to preview the entire test before you begin working problems. Look also for these items:

- how much time you have
- number of questions
- kinds of questions

Now preview the sample math test on the next page.

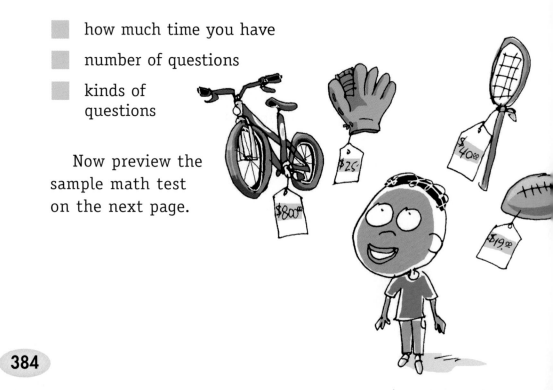

Math Test

PREVIEW

Time limit

Time: 20 minutes

Directions: Read and work each problem. Circle the letter of the correct answer.

PREVIEW

Directions

1. You have 87¢. You buy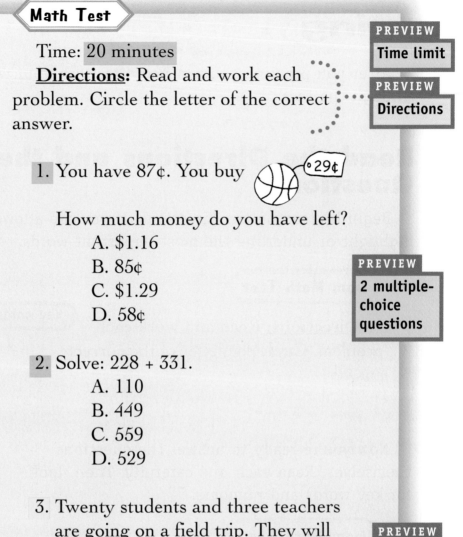

   How much money do you have left?
   A. $1.16
   B. 85¢
   C. $1.29
   D. 58¢

PREVIEW

2 multiple-choice questions

2. Solve: 228 + 331.
   A. 110
   B. 449
   C. 559
   D. 529

3. Twenty students and three teachers are going on a field trip. They will take the school's vans, which hold ten people each. How many vans in all will they need? Show your work.

PREVIEW

1 word problem

Tests

During Reading

After you preview, you can begin to work your way through the test.

Read the Directions and the Questions

Begin by reading the directions. If you are allowed, highlight or underline the most important words.

from Math Test

Key words

Directions: Read and work each problem. Circle the letter of the correct answer.

Now you're ready to answer the questions themselves. Read each one carefully. Then, look for key words and numbers.

from Math Test

1. You have 87¢. You buy

29¢

Key numbers

How much money do you have left?
A. $1.16
B. 85¢
C. $1.29
D. 58¢

Key words

Decide How to Solve the Problem

Use the key words to help you decide how to solve each problem. Ask yourself, "What do I need to find out? Should I add, subtract, multiply, or divide?" The reading strategy of thinking aloud can help.

Think Aloud

The first question is how much money is left. That means I need to subtract. I know I started with 87¢. I bought a ball that cost 29¢. To solve the problem, I have to subtract 29 from 87. I need to line up the numbers.

Do the Math

Now it's time to solve the problem. Work through the problem below and then the one on the next page.

from Math Test

1. You have 87¢. You buy [basketball] ⓞ29¢

   How much money do you have left?
   A. $1.16
   B. 85¢
   C. $1.29
   D. 58¢

$$\begin{array}{r} \overset{7\ 1}{\cancel{8}7} \\ -\ 29 \\ \hline 58 \end{array}$$

Tests

2. Solve: 228 + 331.

Key numbers

A. 110
B. 449
C. 559
D. 529

In this problem, your directions are clear. This is an addition problem. You just need to add the numbers and check your answer. Use a Think Aloud for this problem too.

Think Aloud

First, I'll line up the problem and then solve it. I'll start with the ones column like we do in class.

```
  228
+ 331
  559
```

My answer is 559. That means the correct answer is C. I can check that by subtracting.

```
  559
- 331
  228
```

Yes, that works. 228 is the first number in the problem. I'm sure C is the right answer.

Do Hard Problems Last

Good test-takers often save the hardest problems for last. They also know that most problems are not as tough as they first seem. The key is to read and reread. Take time to let the key facts sink in.

Take this question, for example. What are the key words in this word problem?

> from Math Test
>
> **Key words**
>
> 3. Twenty students and three teachers are going on a field trip. They will take the school's vans, which hold ten people each. How many vans in all will they need? Show your work.
>
> **Directions**

First, be sure you understand the question. Focus on what the question is asking you to find.

> Think Aloud

This problem has two parts. First, I have to figure out how many people are going on the trip. Then, I have to figure out how many vans are needed for that many people. I need to show my work.

Tests

You may want to make a sketch to find the right answer.

20 + 3 = 23 people. I'll draw 1 van and put 10 people in it. I'll draw another van and put 10 people in that van. I know that 10 + 10 is 20. This means that 3 people are left. So I need a third van. The answer is 3.

I can check my answer by subtracting.

```
     23
  - 10—van 1
     13
```

I'll subtract the people in a second van.

```
     13
  - 10—van 2
      3
```

That leaves 3 people. I need a third van for them. My answer of 3 is correct.

After Reading

After you finish a test, look back over the questions and answers. Follow these tips.

- Make sure you didn't skip over any questions.
- Be sure you copied the numbers correctly. Look for careless mistakes in your math.
- Check that you have followed directions and that your answers are easy to read.

Summing Up

- **Prepare for any test or quiz in advance. Find out as much as you can about what kind of questions will be on it.**
- **When you preview, notice the kinds of questions.**
- **Read the directions and questions carefully.**
- **Look for key words that help you decide how to solve the problem.**
- **Use visualizing and thinking aloud to solve the problem.**
- **Check your answers.**

Tests

Reader's
Almanac

- **Strategy Handbook**
- **Reading Tools**
- **Word Workshop**

Strategy Handbook

A reading strategy is a way of getting the information you want when you read. You will want to use different strategies for different kinds of readings.

This part of your *Reader's Handbook* explains six important reading strategies. They are used throughout the handbook.

Think of a strategy as a kind of plan. A coach uses a strategy to help a team win a championship. You can use reading strategies to help you understand more about what you read.

Key Strategies

Almanac

Note-taking

You cannot remember everything you read. That's why you need to take notes. Use a simple list or fill in a chart. Just writing something down can help you remember it. Note-taking works well with all kinds of readings. Try different kinds of notes to see what works best for you.

Here are two kinds of notes.

1. Key Word Notes

Make Key Word Notes when you want to keep track of important topics and ideas in your reading. Divide a notebook page into two columns. List the key word on the left. On the right, write details you want to remember.

Here is an example of Key Word Notes.

Key Word Notes

KEY WORDS	NOTES FROM "STORMS"
hurricane	big storm that forms over warm ocean water
blizzard	cold snowstorm with heavy snow and lots of wind

2. 5 W's and H Organizer

A 5 W's and H Organizer keeps track of the *who, what, when, where, why,* and *how.* When you find key details as you read, write your notes in each box. Here is an example.

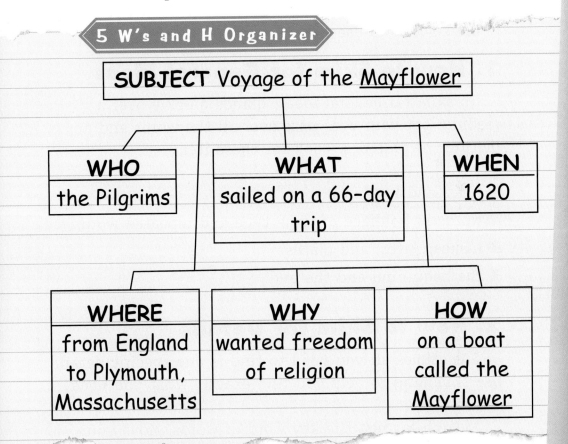

5 W's and H Organizer

SUBJECT Voyage of the <u>Mayflower</u>

| **WHO** the Pilgrims | **WHAT** sailed on a 66-day trip | **WHEN** 1620 |

| **WHERE** from England to Plymouth, <u>Massachusetts</u> | **WHY** wanted freedom of religion | **HOW** on a boat called the <u>Mayflower</u> |

DEFINITION

Note-taking means writing down important details you learn in a class or from a reading. Writing down information about your reading helps you understand and remember it.

Almanac

Skimming

When you skim something, you don't read every word. Instead, you look quickly at the words and pictures. The purpose of skimming is to get a quick idea of what's on the page or to find a certain part.

Here's how to use the strategy of skimming.

1. How to Skim for General Ideas

To skim for general ideas, glance quickly over a reading. Let your eyes pass over all the words and any pictures or graphics. Look for these items:

- titles and headings
- words in boldface or large type and repeated words
- names, dates, and places
- the beginning and the end

2. How to Skim for Details

Sometimes all you need to find is one specific detail. Use skimming to help you find exactly what you need.

Search for just the key word or words. Move your eyes quickly over each paragraph to find what you need. Ignore everything else. When you find the word you're looking for, stop. Read that part carefully.

3. How to Skim for Tests

First, look for the key words in the question. They will tell you what information you need to find. Here's an example.

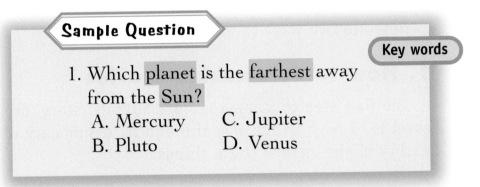

Sample Question

Key words

1. Which planet is the farthest away from the Sun?
   A. Mercury   C. Jupiter
   B. Pluto   D. Venus

The most important words in the question are *planet, farthest,* and *Sun.* Go back to the reading. Skim to find these three words. Read the parts where these words appear to answer the question. You can also skim the reading for the names of the planets in the answers. It's easy to skim for names, because they begin with a capital letter. They will be easy to find.

DEFINITION

Skimming means glancing through a selection. When you skim, you look for key words or a certain part instead of reading every sentence.

Almanac

Summarizing

DESCRIPTION

When you summarize, you retell the main ideas, events, or facts in your own words. The key to summarizing is picking out only the key points.

Here are two ways to use this strategy.

1. How to Summarize Stories

The first step to summarizing a folktale, story, or novel is to read all the way through it. A summary of a story might include these things:

- title and author
- who it's about and where it takes place
- what happens in the beginning, middle, and end

Here's an example of a Story Organizer.

Story Organizer

CHICKEN SUNDAY BY PATRICIA POLACCO

BEGINNING	MIDDLE	END
Three children want to buy a special hat for Miss Eula.	They don't have the money. The shop owner gets angry.	They give the shop owner a present and earn the money.

2. How to Summarize Nonfiction Writing

You can also summarize nonfiction—such as textbooks, articles, biographies, or graphics. You need to be able to sort out what's important from what isn't.

In textbooks, use chapter titles or headings to help you figure out the most important facts. Read the first sentence of every paragraph. Then ask yourself, "What is the author saying?" Watch for words or names that are repeated. Look at vocabulary words that are defined or in bold. Write notes about these important ideas.

Here is an example of Summary Notes.

Summary Notes

KINDS OF GOVERNMENT
1. Community—led by the mayor
2. State—led by the governor
3. National—led by the president

DEFINITION

Summarizing means telling the main events, facts, or ideas in your own words.

Almanac

Using Graphic Organizers

Graphic organizers are "word pictures." They organize information so that it's easy to remember. They help you "see" what an author is saying.

Here are two ways to use graphic organizers.

1. Organizers for Fiction

Graphic organizers are a great way to keep track of details about plot, setting, and characters.

Here's an example of a Story String.

Story String

DOCTOR DE SOTO GOES TO AFRICA
BY WILLIAM STEIG

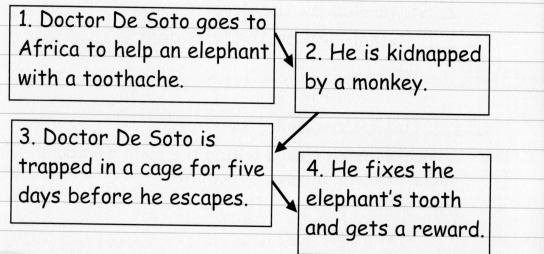

1. Doctor De Soto goes to Africa to help an elephant with a toothache.

2. He is kidnapped by a monkey.

3. Doctor De Soto is trapped in a cage for five days before he escapes.

4. He fixes the elephant's tooth and gets a reward.

2. Organizers for Nonfiction

A chapter in a textbook or an article in a magazine or newspaper is loaded with facts. Use graphic organizers to sort out key details. They can help you put events in order, understand cause and effect, and compare and contrast different things.

Here's an example of a Cause-Effect Organizer.

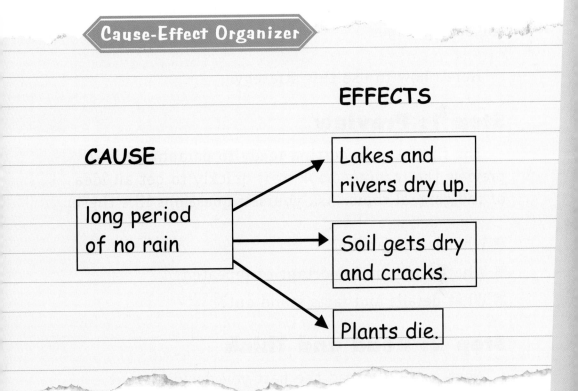

Cause-Effect Organizer

EFFECTS

CAUSE

long period of no rain → Lakes and rivers dry up.

→ Soil gets dry and cracks.

→ Plants die.

DEFINITION

Graphic organizers are word pictures. They are diagrams, charts, and webs that help you understand and remember what you read.

Using Your Own Words

DESCRIPTION

Try to put what you read into your own words. It is a good way to test how well you understand something. When you use your own words to tell about something you read, you are *paraphrasing*.

This strategy works well with stories, nonfiction, poems, maps, graphs, diagrams, and pictures. The key is to choose something short or a small part of something larger.

Here's how to use this strategy.

Step 1: Preview

The first step in getting ready to paraphrase is to preview the reading. Look at it quickly to get an idea of the general topic. Ask yourself questions like these.

- What is this about?
- What words are important or repeated?
- What details and facts stand out?

Step 2: Read and Think

Next, carefully read the part you decide to put into your own words. If you can, circle or highlight important words or phrases. To yourself, talk through what it means. Explain the meaning sentence by sentence or line by line.

Step 3: Put It in Your Own Words

When you are sure you understand the meaning, try to write down the ideas in your own words. What you write should sound like you.

Here is an example of using your own words.

◀ **Double-entry Journal** ▶

TITLE "At the Seaside"	
AUTHOR Robert Louis Stevenson	
QUOTE	MY WORDS

"When I was down
      beside the sea
A wooden spade they
      gave to me
To dig the sandy shore."
	When I was on the beach, they gave me a wood shovel so I could play in the sand.

DEFINITION

Using your own words means finding a way to tell about what you have read by talking through it. Put the author's ideas into words and sentences of your own.

Visualizing and Thinking Aloud

DESCRIPTION

When you visualize something, you make a picture of it. It could be a picture you make in your mind. Or, it could be a drawing or sketch on paper. Thinking aloud means talking to yourself about what you're thinking. Visualizing and thinking aloud works especially well for word problems.

Here's a model of how to use visualizing and thinking aloud with a math problem.

Sample Word Problem

This menu shows 2 kinds of crusts and 3 kinds of toppings. You can choose 1 kind of crust and 1 topping for each pizza. How many different kinds of pizza can be made?

PIZZA MENU

CRUST
(thin or thick)

TOPPINGS
(pepperoni, sausage, or extra cheese)

Step 1: Read and Talk Through the Problem

Read the word problem carefully. Be sure you understand what you need to find out. Talk through the facts you need to get the answer.

Step 2: Make a Sketch

Make a quick drawing to help you solve the problem.

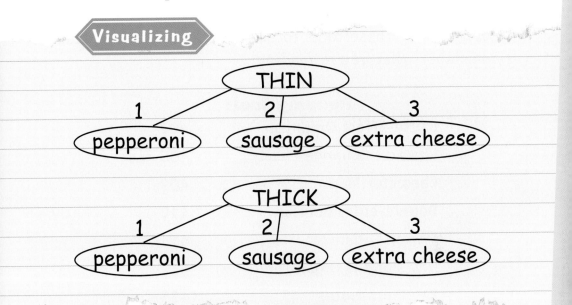

Step 3: Think and Reflect

Take another look at what you drew. Explain it to yourself and check that what you did still makes sense.

Think Aloud

Now I see that there could be 3 kinds of thin crust and 3 kinds of thick crust. So 3 + 3 = 6.

DEFINITION

Visualizing and thinking aloud means making a picture in your mind or on paper. Then talk through your ideas about what you're reading.

Almanac

Reading Tools

Think of this part of the handbook as your reading toolbox. Use these tools to help you keep track of and remember what you're reading.

CAUSE-EFFECT ORGANIZER

A Cause-Effect Organizer helps you to see causes and their effects. You might read about the causes first, followed by effects. Or, you might first read about the effects, followed by causes.

A *cause* makes something happen. An *effect* is the result. Use a Cause-Effect Organizer to show how one thing causes something else to happen.

1. Draw two boxes. Label one CAUSE and the other EFFECT. Draw an arrow to connect them.

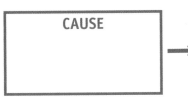

CAUSE		EFFECT

2. As you read, write details in each box. Sometimes you may have more than one cause or effect.

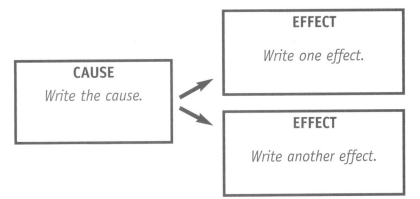

CAUSE
Write the cause.

EFFECT
Write one effect.

EFFECT
Write another effect.

See an example on page 137.

Almanac

CHARACTER CHANGE CHART

Use a Character Change Chart to show how a character grows and changes from the beginning to the end of a story, folktale, or novel. Knowing how a character changes can help you understand a lesson or theme.

1. Make three boxes in a row. Label one BEGINNING, one MIDDLE, and one END.

BEGINNING	MIDDLE	END

2. In each box, write details about what the character is like. Add a box underneath, and label it THEME.

BEGINNING	MIDDLE	END
Write what the character is like at the beginning.	*Write what the character is like in the middle.*	*Write what the character is like at the end.*

THEME	*Write your ideas about the theme or lesson.*

See an example on page 318.

CHARACTER MAP

Use a Character Map to help you remember details about a character from a story or novel.

1. Write the character's name in a small box in the middle. Then make 4 bigger boxes around it.

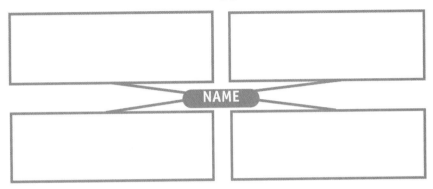

NAME

2. Label each box as shown below. Write specific details about the character in the boxes.

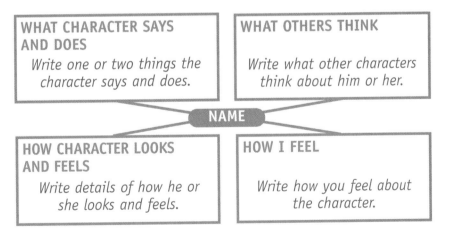

WHAT CHARACTER SAYS AND DOES

Write one or two things the character says and does.

WHAT OTHERS THINK

Write what other characters think about him or her.

NAME

HOW CHARACTER LOOKS AND FEELS

Write details of how he or she looks and feels.

HOW I FEEL

Write how you feel about the character.

See an example on page 288.

DOUBLE-ENTRY JOURNAL

A Double-entry Journal helps you take a closer look at a small part of a reading. Use it to restate a couple of lines in your own words or to react to the writer's ideas.

1. Draw a line through the middle of your paper. Make two columns. Label the first column QUOTES. Label the second column MY WORDS.

QUOTES	MY WORDS

2. When you find a key quote or an important part of a reading, write it in the first column. Then, write your own thoughts about it in the second column.

QUOTES	MY WORDS
Write a key quote or line.	*Write your ideas about it. Use your own words to tell what it means.*

See an example on page 298.

FICTION ORGANIZER

Use a Fiction Organizer to help you remember the details of a story or novel.

1. Draw a small, long box and label it TITLE. Then make three larger boxes that connect to it.

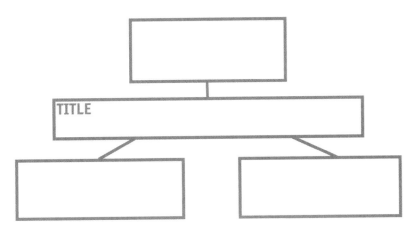

TITLE

2. Label one box CHARACTERS, one SETTING, and one PLOT. Write important details you want to remember in each one.

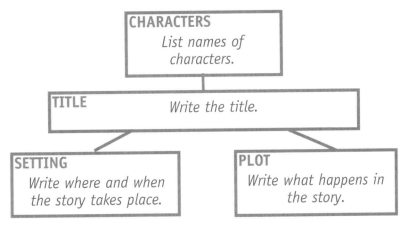

CHARACTERS
List names of characters.

TITLE   *Write the title.*

SETTING
Write where and when the story takes place.

PLOT
Write what happens in the story.

See an example on page 281.

5 W'S AND H ORGANIZER

You can use a 5 W's and H Organizer to keep track of key information about a subject. It helps you organize details about *who, what, when, where, why,* and *how.*

1. Make a small box at the top of your paper. Write SUBJECT here. Then make six boxes below it.

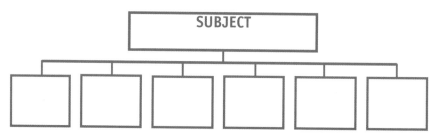

2. Next, label each box with one of these words: *WHO, WHAT, WHEN, WHERE, WHY,* and *HOW.*

3. As you read, fill in the boxes. Try to answer questions that begin with these words.

■ *Who* is this about?   ■ *Where* does this happen?
■ *What* is happening?   ■ *Why* does it happen?
■ *When* does this take place?   ■ *How* does it happen?

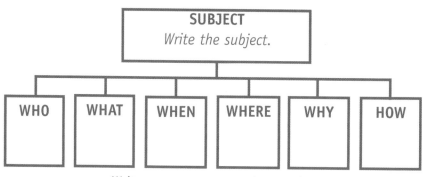

Write an answer to each question.

See an example on page 149.

KEY WORD NOTES

Key Word Notes help you pick out the important words or topics from a reading. They work well for many kinds of reading—from articles and information books to textbooks and biographies.

1. Divide your paper into two columns. Make the right side wider than the left side. Label the left column KEY WORDS. Label the other side NOTES.

KEY WORDS	NOTES

2. As you read, write the most important words or topics in the left column. List details in the right column. These are the big ideas and facts to remember.

KEY WORDS	NOTES
Write the most important words or topics to remember.	*Take notes about each word or topic.*

See an example on page 160.

Almanac

K-W-L CHART

A K-W-L Chart helps you organize what you already know about a subject and decide what you want to find out. It also gives you a place to list the main things you have learned.

1. Get your K-W-L Chart ready before you start to read. Divide your paper into three columns.

2. Label the first column WHAT I **K**NOW. Label the middle column WHAT I **W**ANT TO KNOW. Label the last column WHAT I **L**EARNED.

WHAT I **K**NOW	WHAT I **W**ANT TO KNOW	WHAT I **L**EARNED

3. Before you start reading, fill in the first two columns. After you have finished reading, write down what you learned.

WHAT I **K**NOW	WHAT I **W**ANT TO KNOW	WHAT I **L**EARNED
Write down what you already know about the topic.	*Write two to three questions you have about a topic.*	*List important details and answers to your questions.*

See an example on page 220.

MAIN IDEA ORGANIZER

A Main Idea Organizer helps you do two things:

▪ find the most important idea
▪ keep track of smaller details

1. First, make two boxes. Label the top one SUBJECT and the next one MAIN IDEA. Underneath, make three more boxes. Label each one DETAIL.

SUBJECT		
MAIN IDEA		
DETAIL	DETAIL	DETAIL

2. As you read, look for information to fill in each box.

3. Sometimes, you can tell the main idea right away. Other times, you may need to start by listing the details and decide on the main idea later.

SUBJECT *Write the subject here.*		
MAIN IDEA *Write the author's main point here.*		
DETAIL *Write the first detail.*	DETAIL *Write another detail.*	DETAIL *Write another detail.*

See an example on page 152.

Almanac

PLOT DIAGRAM

A Plot Diagram helps you understand the action of a story or novel. It helps you see what the main problem is, how the action builds to a climax, and how the problem is solved at the end.

1. Make three boxes and connect them with arrows. Put one at the top, one below on the left, and one below on the right. Label them as shown below.

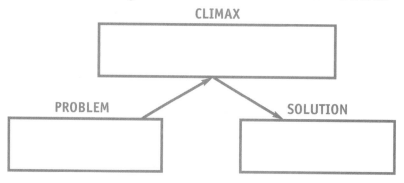

2. As you read, fill in each box with the key details from that part of the story.

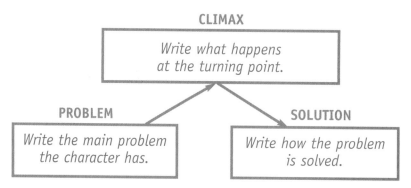

See an example on page 312.

PROCESS NOTES

Process Notes help you keep track of a series of steps or events. They are especially useful when you need to understand how things grow or change, how something works, or how to do something.

1. Make a series of boxes on your page, one below the other. Label the first one SUBJECT. Number the other ones.

SUBJECT

1.

2. For each separate step you read about, make and fill in a new box. Draw arrows to show how one step connects to the next.

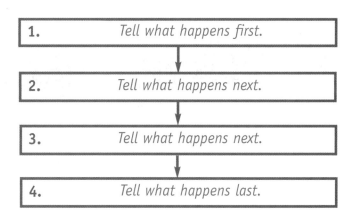

See an example on page 229.

SETTING CHART

Use a Setting Chart to help you remember when and where a story takes place.

1. Make a box at the top of your page. Label it TITLE. Underneath make two big boxes. Label the box on the left CLUES ABOUT TIME. Label the box on the right CLUES ABOUT PLACE.

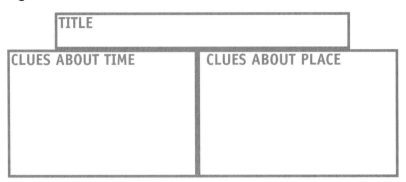

2. Pay attention to details about time and place as you read. Use them to fill in boxes.

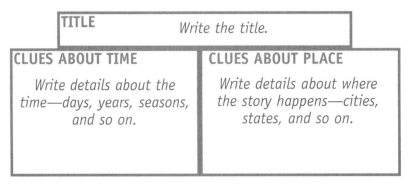

See an example on page 322.

STORYBOARD

A Storyboard uses words and pictures to help you remember what happens in a story or novel.

1. Make three or four big boxes. Number each one. Make a smaller box underneath each one.

1.	2.	3.

2. In each big box, make a simple drawing of an important event in the story. Below, write a sentence about what you drew. Make as many boxes as there are important events.

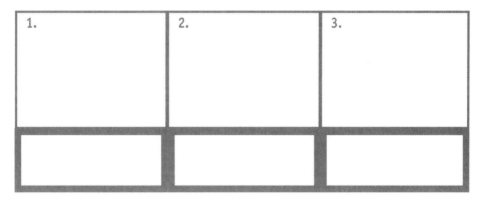

1.	2.	3.
Draw what happens first here.	*Draw what happens next here.*	*Draw the last event here.*
Tell about what you drew.	*Tell about what you drew.*	*Tell about what you drew.*

See an example on page 293.

STORY ORGANIZER

Use a Story Organizer when you want to tell what happens in a story.

1. Make a box at the top and label it TITLE. Then make three big boxes under it. Label the first box BEGINNING, the second box MIDDLE, and the last box END.

TITLE		
BEGINNING	MIDDLE	END

2. Write the main events in each part of the story inside the boxes.

TITLE	*Write the title.*	
BEGINNING	MIDDLE	END
Write what happens first here.	*Write what happens in the middle of the story here.*	*Write how the story ends here.*

See an example on page 311.

STORY STRING

A Story String helps you keep track of the different events that happen in a story or novel. Use a Story String to help you remember the order of events.

1. Write TITLE in a box at the top of your paper. Make at least three boxes underneath. Number each one. Draw arrows to connect them.

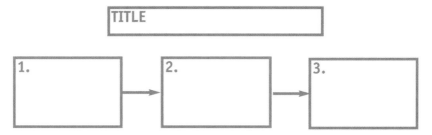

2. Write an important event in each box. Keep adding boxes as you need them.

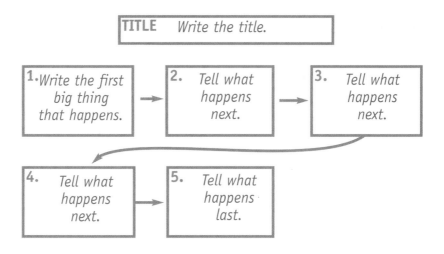

See an example on page 276.

SUMMARY NOTES

Summary Notes help you remember the most important parts of a reading. You can write a summary of a page, a chapter, or even a book.

1. Make a box at the top of your paper. Label it SUBJECT. Then make a big box below it.

SUBJECT

2. After you have finished reading, ask yourself, "What are the most important things for me to remember?" Write them in the box. You may want to number them.

SUBJECT	*Write the subject.*
List three to four important words, ideas, facts, or details.	
1.	
2.	
3.	

See an example on page 178.

TIMELINE

A Timeline lists events in the order they happened. Use a Timeline when you want to remember *what* happened and *when* it happened.

1. Make a box and label it SUBJECT at the top of your page. Then, draw a long straight line or arrow going across the paper.

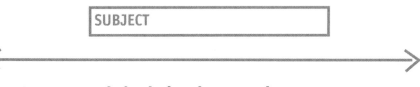

2. As you read, look for dates and events to put on your Timeline. Make a small dot or mark on the line. Write the date above the mark. Write what happened then in the box below. Continue to add dates and boxes as you read.

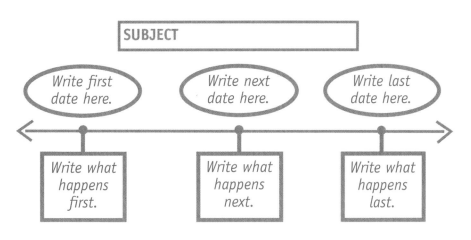

See an example on page 165.

VENN DIAGRAM

A Venn Diagram helps you compare and contrast two things. Use it to understand how two things are the same or different.

1. Draw two big circles on your paper. Make them overlap, as in the drawing below. Shade in the part that overlaps. Write the first item you are comparing at the top of the circle on the left. Write the second item you are comparing on the top of the circle on the right.

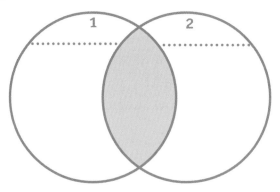

2. As you read, look for ways the two things are the same or different.

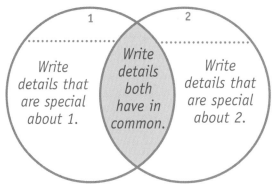

See an example on page 139.

WEB

A Web is a simple tool for taking notes. Use it to organize information, brainstorm ideas, and remember details.

1. Make a box in the center of your paper. Label it SUBJECT. It could be a name, an event, or an idea. Draw two circles near the box, and connect them to the subject.

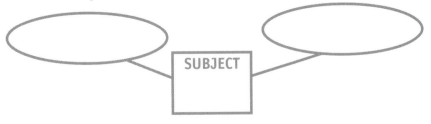

2. Write details or words that relate to your subject in each circle. You might have just two or three circles, or you might have many more.

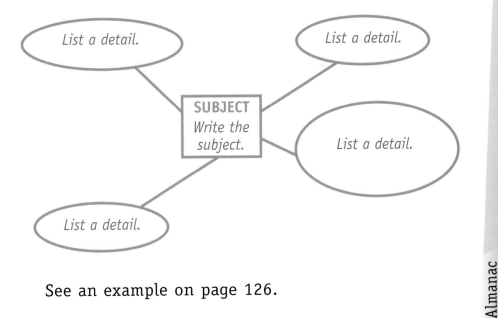

See an example on page 126.

WEBSITE CARD

Use a Website Card to help you take notes on a website. It helps you decide how good the site is and remember what it's about.

1. Make a box and label it NAME AND ADDRESS. Underneath make two boxes. Label one WHAT IT SAYS. Label the other box MY REACTION.

NAME AND ADDRESS
WHAT IT SAYS
MY REACTION

2. Fill in details about the website in each box.

NAME AND ADDRESS
Write the name of the website and its address.
WHAT IT SAYS
Write important facts and details.
MY REACTION
Write your thoughts about the website.

See an example on page 179.

Word Workshop

What do you know about words? Read through this Word Workshop to learn more about letters and sounds, spelling, and word parts.

Letters and Sounds

Learning the sounds that letters make will help you be a better reader. You will read more smoothly, or fluently, and that will help you understand what you read better.

Short Vowels

Vowels can make different sounds. Here are examples of short vowel sounds you can hear in words.

Short *a*	Short *e*	Short *i*	Short *o*	Short *u*
sat	pen	hit	hot	bus
dad	sled	sit	pot	cup
lap	kept	dish	stop	sun
flag	leg	will	shop	duck
apple	best	pick	rock	club

Long Vowels

Long vowels sound similar to the letter name of the vowel. Here are examples of words with long vowel sounds. Note the way the sounds are spelled.

Long *a*	Long *e*	Long *i*	Long *o*	Long *u*
lake	beach	life	note	cute
hay	speed	tie	boat	glue
break	theme	high	know	juice
claim	piece	shy	most	chew
sleigh	seize	buy		(often referred to as words with oo)
	we	eye		

Vowels with *r*

Vowels have different sounds when they are followed by an *r*. Here are some examples.

ar	er	ir	or	ur
c**ar**	moth**er**	g**ir**l	st**or**m	t**ur**n
b**ar**n	read**er**	b**ir**d	b**or**n	s**ur**e
y**ar**d	w**er**e	st**ir**	m**or**ning	p**ur**r

Consonant Clusters

Many words begin or end with a *consonant cluster*. That is a group of two or three consonants. In a cluster, the sounds of each consonant blend together, but you can still hear the different sounds.

Consonants with *r*		Consonants with *l*	
br	**br**ush	*bl*	**bl**ink
cr	**cr**ush	*cl*	**cl**ean
dr	**dr**ive	*fl*	**fl**oor
fr	**fr**esh	*gl*	**gl**ass
gr	**gr**ow	*pl*	**pl**ease
pr	**pr**oud		

Almanac

Consonants with s		Other Beginning Consonant Clusters	
sc	score	scr	scream
sk	sky	shr	shrink
sl	sleep	spr	spring
sm	smile	str	string
sn	sneak	spl	splash
st	steal	thr	through
sw	sweep	tw	twist

Ending Consonant Clusters			
ct	fact	ng	sing
ft	lift	pt	slept
lt	tilt	sk	desk
mp	bump	nt	sent
nd	bend	nce	glance

Consonant Digraphs

A *digraph* is two consonants that make a single sound. Here are some of the most common ones.

Digraph	Beginning	Ending
ch	choose	beach
sh	shout	hush
th	thought	math
wh	where	
tch		catch
nk		drink
ck		back

Phonograms

Phonograms are letter patterns. Knowing about phonograms can help you read and spell new words. If you know how to spell *ate,* you can probably also read and spell *late* or *plate.* Read through these word lists.

Phonograms

ace	face	race	place
ack	back	sack	crack
ade	fade	made	blade
ail	mail	pail	tail
ain	pain	rain	brain
air	hair	pair	stair
ake	lake	cake	take
ale	sale	tale	whale
ame	came	game	name
ank	bank	sank	drank
ap	cap	tap	flap
ark	bark	dark	park
ash	cash	crash	smash
ate	late	gate	plate
aw	jaw	paw	claw
ay	day	may	way
each	beach	teach	reach
eak	leak	weak	speak
eal	deal	meal	steal
ear	dear	hear	year
eat	beat	neat	seat
eed	feed	seed	bleed
een	queen	teen	green
ell	bell	fell	tell
end	send	lend	mend

ent	bent	sent	went
est	best	nest	rest
ew	new	chew	flew
ice	mice	nice	price
ick	kick	sick	thick
ide	hide	side	pride
ight	light	night	tight
in	fin	pin	thin
ine	dine	mine	nine
ink	pink	sink	drink
int	hint	mint	print
ip	dip	chip	grip
it	hit	knit	split
ock	dock	knock	sock
oist	hoist	joist	moist
oke	joke	broke	spoke
one	bone	phone	stone
oop	hoop	scoop	troop
op	hop	pop	drop
ope	hope	rope	slope
ore	more	sore	wore
ound	found	pound	sound
own	town	brown	crown
ub	cub	rub	tub
uck	duck	luck	truck
udge	budge	fudge	judge
ug	dug	rug	tug
ump	bump	dump	jump
unch	lunch	punch	crunch
unk	junk	sunk	trunk
ush	hush	rush	brush

Spelling

Spelling and reading go together. Being good at one helps you do the other.

Commonly Misspelled Words

This spelling list includes many of the words you'll see when you read and use when you write.

Commonly Misspelled Words

a lot	having	piece	tired
about	heard	president	to
always	here	probably	together
April	he's	question	too
are	instead	receive	tried
August	its	remember	Tuesday
author	it's	right	two
because	January	rough	usually
beginning	knew	said	wear
believe	knife	Saturday	weather
buy	knot	school	Wednesday
can't	know	separate	were
children	laugh	September	we're
country	library	special	where
December	making	surprise	whether
different	neighbor	taught	which
doesn't	November	that's	witch
either	o'clock	their	with
enough	often	there	women
especially	once	they're	write
except	our	though	wrote
favorite	own	thought	your
February	people	Thursday	you're

Silent Letters

Many words in English have *silent letters*. Here are some examples of common words with silent letters.

Silent *e*		Silent Consonants	
a with silent e	n*a*me	b	clim**b**
e with silent e	*e*ve	g	**g**nat
i with silent e	l*i*fe	h	g**h**ost
o with silent e	h*o*me	k	**k**new
u with silent e	bl*ue*	l	ta**l**k
		t	lis**t**en
		w	**w**rite

Contractions

A *contraction* is one word made from two longer words. Use an apostrophe to replace the letter or letters you leave out.

Contractions			
am	**have**	**is**	**not**
I'm	I've	here's	aren't
	they've	he's	can't
are	we've	it's	couldn't
they're	you've	she's	didn't
we're		that's	doesn't
you're	**will**	there's	don't
	I'll	what's	hadn't
had, would	he'll	where's	hasn't
I'd	she'll	who's	haven't
it'd	they'll		isn't
she'd			shouldn't
they'd			wouldn't
we'd			

Adding *s* or *es*

The suffixes **s** and **es** are added to nouns to make them plural. Here are rules for forming plurals.

Adding *s* or *es*

1. **Most nouns simply add s.**

   trick   tricks   cloud   clouds

2. **Nouns that end in s, ss, ch, sh, x, and z usually add es. Nouns that end in f usually change f to v and add es.**

   bus   buses   life   lives

3. **Nouns that end in y usually change y to i and add es. Nouns that end in a vowel and y usually just add s.**

   city   cities   toy   toys

4. **Some nouns have unusual (irregular) plurals.**

   man   men   mouse   mice

5. **Some nouns do not change. The singular and the plural forms are the same.**

   deer   deer   sheep   sheep

Adding *ed* or *ing*

The suffixes *ed* and *ing* are added to verbs. Here are examples of the way some verbs change their spelling when these endings are added.

1. Most verbs that end in a consonant simply add *ed* to show that something happened in the past. They also can add *ing*.

help	help*ed*	help*ing*
plant	plant*ed*	plant*ing*

2. Most verbs that end in the vowel *e* usually drop the *e* and add *ed* or *ing*.

love	lov*ed*	lov*ing*
hope	hop*ed*	hop*ing*

   But, for most one-syllable words that end in a consonant, double the consonant before adding *ed* or *ing*.

hop	hop*ped*	hop*ping*
tag	tag*ged*	tag*ging*

3. Many verbs have irregular forms. You have to remember the other forms of these words.

break	broke	breaking
feel	felt	feeling
fight	fought	fighting
go	went	going

Adding *er* or *est*

The suffixes *er* and *est* are often added to describing words called adjectives. These suffixes show that one thing is compared to another.

1. Many adjectives add *er* to show that one thing is compared to another.

brown	brown*er*
soft	soft*er*
light	light*er*
tall	tall*er*

2. Many adjectives add *est* when something is compared to two or more things.

brown	brown*est*
soft	soft*est*
light	light*est*
tall	tall*est*

3. Some adjectives such as *good* and *bad* are unusual. They have different spellings to show when they are used to compare.

good	better	best
bad	worse	worst

Word Parts

Many words are made from at least one prefix or suffix. If you know how these word parts work, you will be able to read and understand many new words.

Prefixes

Prefixes are word parts added to the beginning of a word. When a prefix is added, it changes the meaning of the word. *Happy* means "showing or feeling joy," but *unhappy* means the opposite.

Prefixes	Meanings	Examples
a	not, without	apart, avoid
anti	against	antiwar, antisocial
auto	self	automobile, automatic
bi	two	bilevel, bicycle
co	together	coworker, cooperate
dis	not	disagree, disable
ex	out of, away from	expel, external
il, in	not	illegal, incorrect
inter	between	interstate, interview
micro	small	microwave, microscope
mid	middle	midterm, midtown
non	not, against	nonsense, nonfiction
post	after, later	postscript, postwar
pre	before	prejudge, preview
re	back, again	reappear, return
tri	three	triangle, tricycle
un	not, reverse of	unaware, unsafe
under	below, beneath	underground, underwear

Suffixes

Suffixes are groups of letters (such as **ness**) or a single letter (such as **s**). Suffixes are added to the end of a root word to form new words. Here are some examples of common suffixes.

Suffixes That Form Nouns	Examples
hood	neighborhood, statehood
ist	novelist, artist
ment	judgment, amusement
ness	kindness, happiness
sion	expansion, tension

Suffixes That Form Adjectives	Examples
able	dependable, readable
er	smarter, faster
est	cutest, smartest
ful	painful, hopeful
ish	bluish, childish
less	fearless, mindless

Suffixes That Form Adverbs	Examples
fully	beautifully, carefully
ly	calmly, angrily
ways	sideways, always

Suffixes That Form Verbs	Examples
ed	joked, ripped
en	brighten, eaten
ize	familiarize, sympathize

Almanac

439

Acknowledgments

56-63 From TORNADO by Betsy Byars. Text copyright © 1996 by Betsy Byars. Used by permission of HarperCollins Publishers.

90 From THE KID IN THE RED JACKET by Barbara Park, New York: Alfred A. Knopf.

91, 97 From THE AMERICAN HERITAGE CHILDREN'S DICTIONARY, 1998.

98 From MRS. PIGGLE-WIGGLE by Betty MacDonald, Philadelphia: Lippincott, 1957.

99 From VOLCANO: THE ERUPTION AND HEALING OF MOUNT ST. HELENS by Patricia Lauber, New York: Aladdin Books, 1993.

100 From ALDO ICE CREAM by Johanna Hurwitz, New York: William Morrow and Company, Inc., 1981.

101 From YOUR PET HAMSTER by Elaine Landau, copyright © 1997 by Children's Press. All rights reserved. Reprinted by permission of Children's Press an imprint of Scholastic Library Publishing, Inc.

102 From RAIN FOREST SECRETS by Arthur Dorros. Reprinted by permission of Scholastic, Inc.

103, 119, 254, 256-258, 263, 264 From DISCOVERY WORKS, Level 3 by Badders, et al. Copyright © 2003 by Houghton Mifflin Company. Reprinted by permission of Houghton Mifflin Company. All rights reserved.

104 From I WAS A THIRD GRADE SCIENCE PROJECT by Mary Jane Auch, New York: Holiday House, 1998.

108 From MCBROOM TELLS THE TRUTH by Sid Fleischman. Text copyright © Sid Fleischman. Used by permission of HarperCollins Publishers.

115 From TROMBONES by Bob Temple. Copyright © 2003 by The Child's World, Inc. Reprinted with permission of The Child's World, publisher and copyright holder.

117 From KOALAS by Emilie U. Lepthien. Copyright © 1990 by Children's Press, Inc. Reprinted by permission.

120 From BOOKER T. WASHINGTON by Patricia and Fredrick McKissack, published by Enslow Publishers, Inc. Reprinted by permission.

125 From THE GOLD CADILLAC by Mildred D. Taylor. New York: Dial Books for Young Readers, 1987.

126 From KNIGHTS OF THE KITCHEN TABLE by Jon Scieszka, New York: Viking Penguin, 1991.

127 From WHAT WE CAN DO ABOUT LITTER by Donna Bailey. Copyright © 1991 Franklin Watts. Reprinted by permission.

128 From A TREE IS GROWING by Arthur Dorros. Text copyright © 1997 by Arthur Dorros. Reprinted by permission of Scholastic, Inc.

130 From CYBER SPACE: VIRTUAL REALITY AND THE WORLD WIDE WEB by David Jefferis. Copyright © 1999 by Alpha Communications and Firecrest Books, Ltd. Reprinted by permission of the author.

132 From DINOSAURS BEFORE DARK by Mary Pope Osborne, New York: Random House, 1992.

134 From CROWS! STRANGE AND WONDERFUL Text copyright © 2002 by Laurence Pringle; Illustration copyright © 2002 by Bob Marstall. Published by Boyds Mills Press, Inc. Reprinted by permission.

136 From THE SUPER SCIENCE BOOK OF ROCKS AND SOILS by Robert Snedden, 1995.

138 Reprinted from the May 2002 issue of RANGER RICK magazine, with the permission of the publisher, the National Wildlife Federation. Copyright 2002 by the National Wildlife Federation.

144-145, 148, 150, 152 "Bubble, Bubble, Spittlebug" by Beverly J. Letchworth from HIGHLIGHTS FOR CHILDREN April 2003, Vol. 58, No 4, Issue 618. Copyright © 2003 by Highlights for Children, Inc., Columbus, Ohio. Reprinted by permission.

156, 157, 159-164 Reprinted with permission from BENJAMIN FRANKLIN: PAINTER, INVENTOR, STATESMAN by David A. Adler, © 1992.

156 From BENJAMIN FRANKLIN: PAINTER, INVENTOR, STATESMAN by David A. Adler, illustrated by Lyle Miller, 1992. Reprinted by permission of Holiday House.

168 From GIANT PANDAS by Patricia A. Fink Martin. © 2002 by Children's Press. Reprinted by permission.

170 From GIANT PANDAS: GIFTS FROM CHINA by Alan Fowler. © 1985 by Children's Press. Reprinted by permission.

176-178, 180 Screen captures from www.sandiegozoo.org. All rights reserved. Reprinted by permission.

182, 184, 185, 189, 190 KID'S ALMANAC FOR THE 21ST CENTURY.

191 From ELEANOR EVERYWHERE: THE LIFE OF ELEANOR ROOSEVELT by Monica Kulling, copyright © 1999 by Monica Kulling. Illustrations © 1999 by Cliff Spohn. Used by permission of Random House Children's Books, a division of Random House, Inc.

194 From THE WORLD BOOK ENCYCLOPEDIA. © 2003 World Book, Inc. By permission of the publisher, www.worldbook.com.

195 From AMAZING FLYING MACHINES by Robin Kerrod. Copyright © Dorling Kindersley Ltd. 1992. Reprinted by permission of Penguin Books Ltd.

196 www.sportlines.com

197 From PENGUINS by Judith Jango-Cohen, New York: Benchmark Books, Marshall Cavendish Corporation, 2002.

202 From THE PRESIDENCY by Patricia J. Murphy. Reprinted by permission of Compass Point Books. Text copyright © 2002 Compass Point Books.

204 Reprinted from the November 2003 section of RANGER RICK'S *Go Wild!* Web site, with the permission of the publisher, the National Wildlife Federation.

205 From www.whitehouse.gov/kids. Reprinted by permission.

210-213, 218, 219 From COMMUNITIES: ADVENTURES IN TIME AND PLACE by J. Banks, et al. Copyright © 2001, 2000, 1999 McGraw-Hill School Division, a Division of the Educational and

Professional Publishing Group of The McGraw-Hill Companies, Inc. Reproduced by permission of The McGraw-Hill Companies.

224-227, 231, 232, 266 From HARCOURT SCIENCE, Pupil's Edition, Grade 3, copyright © 2002 by Harcourt, Inc., reprinted by permission of the publisher.

236, 237, 239, 241, 243 From HOUGHTON MIFFLIN MATHEMATICS, Level 3 by Vogeli, et al. Copyright © 2002 by Houghton Mifflin Company. Reprinted by permission of Houghton Mifflin Company. All rights reserved.

261, 267 From SHARE OUR WORLD in WE THE PEOPLE by Hartoonian, et al. Copyright © 1997 by Houghton Mifflin Company. Reprinted by permission of Houghton Mifflin Company. All rights reserved.

262, 265 From HARCOURT HORIZONS PEOPLE AND COMMUNITIES, Orlando: Harcourt, Inc., 2003.

272, 273, 277, 278, 280 "The Lion and the Mouse" from AESOP'S FABLES© 2000 by Jerry Pinkney. Used with permission of Chronicle Books LLC, San Francisco. Visit ChronicleBooks.com.

284, 285, 287-289, 291 From FLAT STANLEY by Jeff Brown, illustrated by Steve Bjorkma. Text copyright © 1964 by Jeff Brown. Illustrations copyright © Steve Bjorkman. Used by permission of HarperCollins Publishers.

296, 299-302, 304 "Michael Is Afraid of the Storm" from BLACKS by Gwendolyn Brooks. Reprinted by consent of Brooks Permissions.

307-311 From THE SKIRT by Gary Soto. Illustrated by Eric Velasquez, copyright © 1992 by Gary Soto. Illustrations © 1992 by Eric Velasquez. Used by permission of Random House Children's Books, a division of Random House, Inc.

314-317 From JAKE DRAKE KNOW-IT-ALL, by Andrew Clements. Reprinted with the permission of Simon & Schuster Books for Young Readers, an imprint of Simon & Schuster Children's Publishing Division. Text copyright © 2001 Andrew Clements.

321-324 From STONE FOX by John Reynolds Gardiner. Text copyright © 1980 by John Reynolds Gardiner. Used by permission of HarperCollins Publishers.

327 "Flea Fur All" from BING BANG BOING copyright © 1994 by Douglas Florian, reprinted by permission of Harcourt, Inc.

328 From THE STORIES JULIAN TELLS by Ann Cameron, New York: Pantheon Books, 1981.

329 From THE BEE TREE by Patricia Polacco, copyright © 1993 by Patricia Polacco. Used by permission of Philomel Books, a division of Penguin Young Readers Group, a Member of Penguin Group (USA) Inc., 345 Hudson St., New York, NY 10014. All rights reserved.

330 From CHARLOTTE'S WEB by E. B. White. New York: HarperCollins, 1952.

332 "When I Was Lost" from ALL TOGETHER by Dorothy Aldis, copyright 1925-1928, 1934, 1939, 1952, renewed 1953, © 1954-1956, 1962 by Dorothy Aldis, © 1967 by Roy E. Porter, renewed. Used by permission of G. P. Putnam's Sons, a division of Penguin Young Readers Group, a Member of Penguin Group (USA) Inc., 345 Hudson St., New York, NY 10014. All rights reserved.

333 From FANTASTIC MR. FOX by Roald Dahl, New York: Penguin Group, 1970.

334 From SQUANTO'S JOURNEY: THE STORY OF THE FIRST THANKSGIVING, Copyright © 2000 by Joseph Bruchac, reprinted by permission of Harcourt, Inc.

335 From SIDEWAYS STORIES FROM WAYSIDE SCHOOL by Louis Sachar, New York: Alfred A. Knopf, 1978.

336 "Pie Problem" from A LIGHT IN THE ATTIC by Shel Silverstein. Copyright © 1981 by Evil Eye Music, Inc. Used by permission of HarperCollins Publishers.

337 "Labor Day" from CELEBRATIONS by Myra Cohn Livingston. Text copyright © 1985 by Myra Cohn Livingston. Used by permission of Marian Reiner.

338 From PLEASING THE GHOST by Sharon Creech, New York: HarperCollins, 1996.

340 "At the Library" by Nikki Grimes. Copyright © 1997 by Nikki Grimes. Published in IT'S RAINING LAUGHTER by Nikki Grimes, originally published by Dial Books for Young Readers. Reprinted by permission of Curtis Brown, Ltd.

341 "Noodles" by Janet S. Wong. Reprinted with permission of Margaret K. McElderry Books, an imprint of Simon & Schuster Children's Publishing Division from GOOD LUCK GOLD AND OTHER POEMS by Janet S. Wong. Copyright © 1994 Janet S. Wong.

342 "The Locked Closet" from THE BUTTERFLY JAR by Jeff Moss, copyright © 1989 by Jeff Moss. Used by permission of Bantam Books, a division of Random House, Inc.

343 From ENCYCLOPEDIA BROWN AND THE CASE OF THE TREASURE HUNT by Donald J. Sobol, New York: William Morrow and Company, Inc., 1988.

344 "I'm Roaring like a Lion" from IT'S RAINING PIGS & NOODLES by Jack Prelutsky. Text copyright © 2000 by Jack Prelutsky. Used by permission of HarperCollins Publishers.

345 "Many People Who Are Smart" from THE SKY IS ALWAYS IN THE SKY, by Karla Kuskin. Text copyright © 1998 by Karla Kuskin. Used by permission of HarperCollins Publishers.

346 From THE GREAT KAPOK TREE, copyright © 1990 by Lynne Cherry, reprinted by permission of Harcourt, Inc.

347 From SPOTLIGHT ON CODY by Betsy Duffey, New York: Viking Penguin, 1998.

PHOTO CREDITS

The editors have made every effort to trace the ownership of all copyrighted selections found in this book and to make full acknowledgment for their use. Omissions brought to our attention will be corrected in a subsequent edition.

Author and Title  Index